CROSSING BRITTANY

Walking the Nantes-Brest Canal

Wendy Mewes

Hic amor, haec patria est

Red Dog Books

CROSSING BRITTANY
Walking the Nantes-Brest Canal
published by Red Dog Books
ISBN 978-0-9557088-2-4

© Wendy Mewes 2008

British Library Cataloguing-in-Publication Data
A catalogue record for this book is available from the British Library

Red Dog Books is based in Axbridge, Somerset and in Brittany.
Enquiries should be addressed to the editorial office at
Red Dog Books, 29410 Plounéour-Ménez, France.

email: reddogbooks@orange.fr

www.reddogbooks.com

Printed by imprint*digital*.net

Caminante, son tus huellas
El camino, y nada más;
Caminante, no hay camino
Se hace camino al andar.
Al andar se hace camino,
Y al volver la vista atrás
Se ve la senda que nunca
Se ha de volver a pisar.
Caminante, no hay camino,
Sino estelas en la mar.

Walker, there is no path
But in your footsteps;
Walker, there is no path:
In walking, you create it.
In walking you make the way,
And in turning to look behind
You see a track
You'll never tread again.
Walker, there is no path
Only traces of foam in the sea.

Antonio Machado

Writer and walker Wendy Mewes lives in the Monts d'Arrée, Finistere. She enjoyed teaching Latin and Ancient History to students aged 8 to 80 in the UK before concentrating on writing and research in Brittany. There she is also president of the Brittany Walks association, which aims to illuminate Breton history and landscape for anglophones through courses and walks. For more information, visit her blog *Brittany Blues* (www.wendymewes.blogspot.com).

Other Books by Wendy Mewes

Discovering the History of Brittany

Red Dog Guide to the Nantes-Brest Canal

Walking and other activities in Finistere

Finistere: Things to see and do at the End of the World

Walking the Brittany Coast: Morlaix to Benodet

Novels

Moon Garden

The Five of Cups

Contents

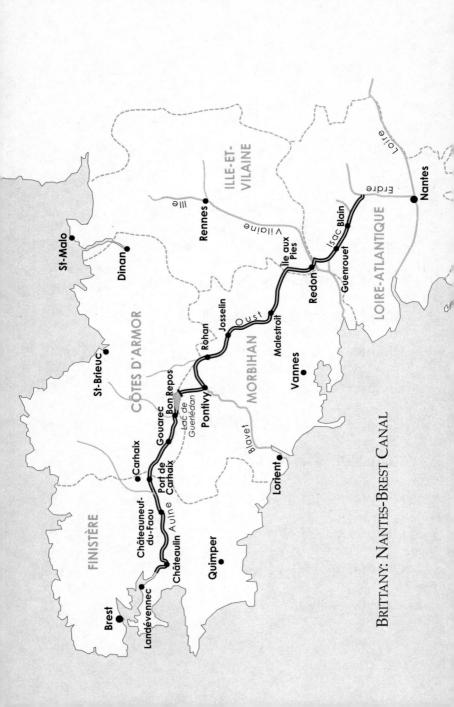

BRITTANY: NANTES-BREST CANAL

Introduction

One End of the Thread

"Never have I been so much myself ... as in journeys I have taken alone and on foot"
Rousseau

My walk along the Nantes-Brest Canal began out of an objective historical interest and turned into a journey of more personal significance. Criss-crossing the canal around Brittany during research for an earlier book some years ago had provoked my curiosity. I began to stop and walk short stretches whenever time allowed: at Josselin in sunshine, near Rostrenen in the snow and during flooding below Châteauneuf-du-Faou. The striking contrasts of appearance and atmosphere in canalised rivers caught my imagination after the narrow, straight channels of the Stroud valley of my childhood.

The canal's route from Nantes - former capital of Brittany but now administratively outside its boundaries - runs right through the departments of Morbihan, Côtes d'Armor and Finistère, crossing the old frontier of the Breton language and the historic heartlands of the west. Its construction redefined the landscape of central Brittany. The courses of seven rivers are harnessed by the canal in its 365km length, the intervening hills traversed by long series of locks to raise and lower the artificial connecting sections. I knew from the moment of tracing its route across a map that I would have to walk the entire length to get to grips with its singular identity as a remaining physical and symbolic link between old and new Brittany.

The idea of completing this long journey in one bite and condensing my experience into a couple of weeks of effort was unappealing. I wanted to see the canal in all its moods, season by season, not just to look at the scenery but to feel its past and evolution, to take the time to get to know its character. Given other writing commitments to be fitted in alongside, a year seemed the perfect timescale for the whole endeavour. What I had not bargained for was that the particularities of canal walking would throw the switch that cast a powerful spotlight on my own notions of identity. Once my awareness of this began, almost from the word Nantes, the project became something of a quest, albeit with an elusive quarry.

The long walk from the - to me - relatively unknown marches of eastern Brittany to my well-loved and familiar territory of Finistère took on the form of a pilgrimage, rather than recreation, with all its attendant mixture of physical pain balanced by spiritual gain. I was to endure torrential downpours and electric storms, suffer the annoyance of blisters and the agonies of shin splints, as well as discovering with a vengeance the tenacious character of what I came to call the long thought. Like learning Breton, the way was to be long and hard but with a beautiful end in view.

The canal was built in the first half of the 19th century. The initial impulse was defensive: with English ships persistently blockading Breton ports and attacking coastal settlements during the Revolutionary and Napoleonic years, a safe inland route to link the arsenals at Nantes and Brest seemed a prudent strategic measure, although in practice this was never the main occupation of the canal. The transport of goods - wood, slate, sand and grains - became its primary economic function, but the competition of faster and more effective methods of transport meant the heyday was to be short-lived. What had seemed visionary in the first proposals of the mid-18th century was parochial in the early 20th, especially after the loss of men, boats and spirit following the Great War. Today much of the canal's length is navigable by pleasure craft, save for a sad central section on each side of Lac de Guerlédan, the latter an engineering feat that severed the canal in the 1920s, making its original purpose redundant.

To travel along this canal today is to take a journey through the history of Brittany, over territory where Bretons and

French fought for control, with interludes of Viking, English, Spanish and German interventions, where men of these and many other nationalities have killed and died for profit, for power and mostly for nothing over many centuries.

Starting in the marshlands, the marais, of the Marches of Brittany, it crosses those most fiercely contested border lands where frequent bloody conflict marked Breton resistance to the inroads of Franks in the 9th century and again in the 20th when Americans shelled the last German positions across the river Isac in 1944. Political and religious conflicts over the centuries are recalled in obvious landmarks like the châateau of Blain and Josselin's imposing castle, both seats of the Rohans, one of the greatest of Breton families, whose members were influential for good or ill in many of the events that shaped the development of Brittany. The mighty Aulne, last river in the grand chain, ends at Landévennec where the abbey was sacked by Vikings in 913, and the entrance to the Rade de Brest, patrolled by U-boats from the German submarine base in Brest during WWII. Such are the contrasts and similarities of historical experience that have left their mark on this complex land.

Walking the canal is both a physical and a psychological experience. It is easy going, eliminating the need for constantly looking down at the feet - an aspect which frees the mind for its own travel - and it is impossible to get lost. Experience over the full length of this route confirmed my instinct that movement not stillness is the most natural state of man. To walk is to measure our physical existence against the natural world, to revive an ancestral memory of the most basic human purpose, to reach something or somewhere. The scenery is allowed to unroll its secrets at the natural pace, on the true human scale, rather than flashing past as when one is in a car or on a bike. The walker is temporarily part of the landscape he traverses, contributing his small sounds, his light imprint to the cyclical whole of nature, passing as animals do, or leaves unfurling and falling with the seasons. There is at the same time both an involvement and a detachment from the landscape.

But walking alone in such an environment also means an inevitably strong engagement with the self. There is no avoiding it. The geography of the canal forces a focus and a discipline that belies the notion of rambling, which is more applicable to open countryside. The very word channel for the watercourse is indicative of this. It lends itself to mental evolution, a slow process of thought development. That movement leads to ideas was a concept promulgated by the itinerant Sophists of classical Greece, who travelled from city to city and festival to festival giving public lectures on rhetoric and philosophy, touting a form of higher education to those who could afford to pay for it. A similar concept came with strolling players who brought theatre to the uneducated in rural villages and hamlets, the stimulation of new thoughts outside the limitations of the daily familiar round. The same was true of the canal, a route of communication, a conduit for the transfer and infiltration of ideas and practices, window on a wider world for the isolated centre of rural Brittany.

The chain of inner reflection fostered by walking the canal is a long one, and this mental awareness inevitably slides sooner or later into the question of identity. Every avenue of thought seems to lead to it. Any study of history provokes subjective judgements and personal comparisons, and my homage to the canal - a fine historical character in its own right - and research into that fabled notion of Breton identity brought me quickly up against assessment of my own place in Brittany and in the wider scheme of being and belonging. Reaching the age of fifty during the stages of my journey perhaps also contributed its part to this tendency.

In practice, it was the death of one of my closest friends soon after work on this book began that led directly to my descent into the long thought. Over ten gruelling years of cancer, a disease that strives for control over the mind as much as the body, her individuality became absorbed and shrunken into the identity of illness. Forced to relinquish the persona of a professional singer, she struggled to substitute a definition of self beyond the defensive role imposed by this engagement in mortal combat. I was thinking a lot about her life, the twists and turns, upheavals and new starts, the constants and the variables, trying to pinpoint the essence of her existence. This goes straight to the minefield of identity, where tip-toeing through the options can be to risk the most basic securities of self. I am this or that, I am here or there, I am something and finally nothing.

The canal itself is a natural metaphor for thought with its varied flow of water, smooth or stagnant, and the locks, symbolic of both obstacle and solution, impeding progress as well as providing keys to unblock the passages of the mind and allow movement from impulse to conclusion. The issue that haunted my journey began with thoughts on national identity, a notion raised by the canal as a connecting link between the historic and 'new' geography of Brittany. But as my work progressed, some surprising answers emerged to the long personal search which has been a recurrent motif of my life from a very early age.

The curious expression 'the English' haunted my childhood. Curious because I was brought up in Gloucestershire, on the Cotswold cusp, the edge of the heart of England. The words were spoken with a sneer, a hint of spittle in my father's mouth. No wonder the world was alien to me, full of these cheaters and twits all brazenly living in their own country, while we, one short step from the valleys of south Wales, grubbed a meagre living from a school-teacher's wages in a foreign land. So I spoke their language, in as unattractive an accent as the next child, but was apparently not one of them. I thought even then that the world was unfair to make me different - what children most fear - in some slight mis-location, perhaps with the supporting evidence of a hot stripe of passion, an ear for words and a rarely fulfilled need for the sea. This was my puzzle: if others were 'the English' then obviously I couldn't be one of them, but then were holidays in Abersoch enough to validate the Welshness of my blood?

Identity is of course a perception and how we see

ourselves is intrinsically bound up with how others see us. It derives from social experience and changes with time and place or laterally with presentation to different people: it is mercurial, fluid and progressive, its appearance like a long, thin balloon which when grabbed acquires new shape by breaking into another form in another place, eluding the compression of its whole. It twists and expands into family, group and national identity, spiralling away from the stark difficulty of the perennial question - not so much who am I, as where do I fit in?

This has remained a difficulty all my life, and it lies at the heart of my attachment to places before people, to my constant urge for travel and mental movement and search for the place of belonging. What I didn't know - and what comfort it would have given me in earlier years - was that the elusive nirvana could be found in a 'foreign' country, and that walking the Nantes-Brest canal would furnish the moment of epiphany.

A search for identity can be exciting, revealing and painful by turns. It has been an issue in Brittany for a very long time, as the bones of language, culture, history and territory are picked over relentlessly, from the relatively harmless airy-fairy celtic-spiral brand of mythology to the pseudo-identity of Breton-named Parisians of the far right and the touristic marketing fake identity of the 'petite cité de caractère' or a fishing village without fishermen. The place of identity is a never-never land for absolute truth.

Chapter 1   Nantes and the Erdre

*"No city should be too large for a man to walk
out of it in a morning"*
Cyril Connolly

The start of my journey is in Nantes, even if a walk along the towpath of the canal does not begin here. I'm taking a few days to get reacquainted with this buoyant city, and test the psychological water for beginning my journey. Anyone setting themselves up for a walk of this length - no matter in what timescale - must be prepared for long thoughts, and I know I'm heading that way: what I don't know is from what direction the assault will come. Before leaving Nantes, I have a pretty good idea.

This former capital, intrinsic limb of the history of Brittany, was sheered off from its natural body by the Vichy government in 1941 and in post-war reorganisation became head of the department of Loire Atlantique, part of Pays de la Loire, in 1957. To many it remains an emotive part of Brittany, and the canal, linking Nantes with the western hinterland, has its symbolic significance in the amoebic concept of Breton identity.

I've never forgotten a painting seen long ago of one of the city's most infamous historical incidents. During the Revolution, the current power faction in Paris in 1793 sent Jean-Baptiste Carrier to put down the Vendéen uprising. His method here was simple - kill anyone who could not demonstrate suitable republican sentiments. When guillotining proved too slow and labour intensive, mass executions by firing squads followed, but when those too failed to keep up with the alarming acceleration of hapless victims, Carrier devised his abominable 'déportations verticales': barge loads of prisoners, men, women and children, often tied together in couples, were sunk in the river Loire, whilst grinning boatmen looked on and pushed the feisty down with boathooks or hacked at the limbs of strugglers with their swords.

The Loire is unromantic, wide and grey, stretching its two arms around the Ile de Nantes, intent on escape into the Atlantic. It once had no less than seven branches flowing through the city before some lamentable decisions about urban planning in the 1930s saw the demise of several islands, to improve navigation and cater for other forms of modern transport. Silting had always been a problem for shipping and many larger vessels were unloaded at Paimboeuf to the west (once linked to Nantes by its own canal). What was the Ile de Feydeau still retains gracious mercantile houses of the 18th century, with their ornamental stone mask-faces, and along the Quai de la Fosse some of the handsomest of this type of establishment now lean drunkenly on their shifting foundations, the characteristic decorative iron balconies at jaunty angles.

The extraordinary 18th century wealth of Nantes, third port in France, was actually built on the less flimsy foundation of human misery: slavery, the 'triangular trade', that saw ships take cheap cargoes to Africa, reload with human beings bound for plantations in the West Indies, and then return to France with spices, sugar and cotton. In the city museum, a rather simplistic symbolism of entrapment and confinement makes rooms dealing with this topic of 'black gold' noticeably more sombre and claustrophobic than the soaring light in evidence elsewhere.

Nantes has a nautical profile: regardless of its inland location 50kms from the Atlantic, water and its commercial exploitation lie at the heart of the city's historic identity despite the loss of such a great proportion of visible manifestation of this with the re-routing and driving underground of Nantes' waterways. A casual visitor today might see the château and cathedral, stroll in the medieval streets and shop in the many chic centres without being in the least aware of the Loire, now kept at bay by tram and railway lines that serve the faster needs of an urban sprawl.

Visiting Nantes is the only time I've had any sense of being in a real city since living in Brittany. As someone who dwelt in fairly central London for many years it brings back a strangely familiar feeling - the pace and rhythm are distinctly different from, say, Brest or even Rennes. Getting into the centre takes a long time: it requires a proper journey through traditionally ugly suburbs, industrial sprawl and out-of-town warehouse units.

Once inside the periphery, and clunking on and off tramlines, there is the sense of this great outer encircling ring, spokes of a wheel rimmed by the essential suburbs and dormitory towns of a great economic centre. But if the urban atmosphere is distinctive, it nevertheless lacks that ubiquitous tension and aggression of the English capital. Nantes feels like a calm and confident city. For all its fine medieval and baroque architecture, it is a modern place, not leisurely - by French standards at least - and the pulse of change, development and adaptability seems to beat close to the surface.

Such themes are made much of in the newly revamped city museum, just opened in the old ducal château, after extensive renovations. The transformation of space and light is imaginatively bright: given it is not possible to conceal a towering lift-shaft in a medieval building, a bold stroke chooses bright red to draw the attention, echoed on a smaller scale in leather chairs and sofas, a keynote colour both congruous and striking. For all the multi-media, multi-lingual exhibits, nooks and crannies of the ancient building have been left bare - and pleasingly unexplained - to retain an authentic sense of irregularity and a stimulus to the historic imagination.

What is odd is that I see not a single reference to the Nantes-Brest canal here, despite much on the Loire and the Brivet. Does this suggest a lack of relevance to the city's identity which is the overall focus of the exhibitions? The canal certainly never brought much in the way of wealth into Nantes so perhaps that's it. But neither did I notice anything on that running sore on the skin of Breton identity - the severance of Nantes from Brittany.

The derivation of the word identity from the Latin *idem* (same) and possibly *identidem* (repeatedly) emphasises the aspect of similarity, of identification with others. This implies a set of core values which override social divisions, and the commonalities of a group. In this sense identity becomes also a separatist notion, because at once a gulf, explicit or implicit, arises between those within the group and those without. The name of the group, whether it is a nationality, political party, social club, or voluntary organisation furnishes a handy label that identifies shared traits or goals. The group is a cloak for the individual, a modus vivendi outside of self.

The issue of Breton identity is important in the distinction it makes in separation from the French, the old aggressive enemy that swallowed up Breton autonomy as readily as it sacrificed Breton man-power in its wars. Despite the negative Paris-generated images of stupidity and stubbornness over the centuries, the Bretons have established a strong reputation throughout the world, maintained their language against all the odds and re-exploited rich veins of tradition to fashion a distinctive living and developing culture. Brittany still retains a strong social cohesion which emanates from its religious past and the closeness of life to the land and sea, both inextricably linked to economy and outlook.

But if group identity of whatever form is cohesive and connecting, identity for the individual means an awareness of differences and some degree of separation. I may be like other members of the various associations I belong to in the sharing of similar interests or beliefs, and I may have much in common in social, economic and educational terms with many other British people here, but my own individuality is unique. It is at those frequent points of *not* marching to the same tune as others that this becomes sharply and sometimes distressingly apparent. I take refuge in the identity that is a creation of the imagination rather than social realism.

The harping on that theme, that very word - identity - is beginning to set off kaleidoscopic movements inside my head. A myriad of tiny pieces are shifting and settling, shifting and settling, forming pattern after pattern of brightly-coloured figures: abstract images of past or potential personae, all fragmentary, both revealing and concealing.

What does my strong visceral reaction to this word have to say about my own sense of identity? This irksome question is one I've been avoiding for a long time, but the concept of being born in one place and yet belonging to another or to nowhere at all is one I've struggled with and physically pursued for much of my life.

In the château museum is the gold reliquary in which the heart of Anne de Bretagne was placed after her death in 1514. This noble lady, married to two kings of France successively, has become over the centuries a sentimental focus of notions of Breton identity. She is attributed with a clear mission to preserve the independence of her duchy, lost in practice by her father François II on the battle field at Saint-Aubin-du-Cormier in 1488. A miracle of merged identity is apparent in the confusion of Anne, mother of Mary, patron saint of Brittany and Anne-de-Bretagne, the good-hearted duchess, loyal to the last to her own land. It seems to me she did what any medieval ruler of sense would do in touring her dominions as a way of cementing popular support.

The struggle over 'ownership' of this reliquary in more modern times is another issue of identity: on display at the Musée Dobrée, it was claimed as the possession of the municipality and shut away in the Hôtel de Ville for many years. Political changes were necessary before the heart could take its place in the new château museum, emphasising its symbolic value for the city of Nantes in the context of Breton ducal history.

Anne de Bretagne's representational importance raises also the thorny issue of language: this paragon of virtue, champion of proud Brittany in the face of arrogant France, did not in fact speak or read Breton. So the archetypal Breton lacks a vital linguistic link, a fundamental form of communication with 'her people'.

I don't speak Welsh, neither did my parents, despite their national pride and sense of a defining identity from their south Wales origins. To what extent is Welshness or Bretonness bound up in language? Can one interpret the true

17

voice of one's native land in the language of its conqueror and oppressor? Many would say not, and many of those would take the high moral ground over this issue.

I was recently invited to sign books at a French/Breton literary festival. It was a mostly agreeable event, with fifteen fellow-authors on subjects varying from food through history to detective stories and poetry. But here I was told imperiously by a Breton writer that I *must* speak Welsh. This was after a long period in which he had subjected me to a tedious monologue about his own particular brand of history. For a moment I thought it was just a pleasantry, but in fact he persisted with chilly seriousness. A more fitting target for his insistence might have been the many non-Breton-speaking Bretons who visited the event that day - presumably they were less Breton than he and therefore of less significance in some indefinable way. These kinds of value judgements are always unpleasant and issued from a point of lofty superiority of 'chosen' group status that soon turns to extremity in the right conditions. In this case, he was missing the fundamental point that language is about communication, and that communication is by definition a two-way process: this was not a skill he had demonstrated in our brief acquaintance. How such a lack of human perception is made up for by a native knowledge of the Breton tongue is beyond me - it thinly disguises the emptiness beneath the rhetoric of cultural extremism. Communication is deeper than language, identity is infinitely more complex than oral expression.

I begin to think on this trip to Nantes of ways in which communication is a crucial facet of identity. Rulers - then and now - have many ways of presenting themselves and of controlling their media. The Roman coins with their portraits I've recently been viewing in one of Nantes' fine museums, the Musée Dobrée, are an obvious example. But so on the level of the individual - aren't we all the time projecting our desired image to others, modifying and reshaping like Proteus with each new audience? When I open my email facility and see the five little figures representing the various personae which I use to communicate with the outside world, I realise that each represents a different and distinct aspect of my self. Those who know me through one might not recognise the same individual in the guise of another. The Portuguese poet Fernando Pessoa wrote prose and poetry under various heteronyms - not pseudonyms, but discrete personalities with their own histories, beliefs, concepts, experiences and linguistic patterns. He simply took to a logical conclusion the realisation that he was both different people and no one person. This is one of the long thoughts that is to haunt my journey.

One of the earliest of the savage blows dealt by the Vikings on Brittany fell on Nantes in 843. A large fleet of long-boats sailed up the Loire and took the city unawares, with most of the population at worship on the feast day of St-Jean. They were slaughtered indiscriminately, including the bishop as he celebrated mass. The cathedral, in which many were taking refuge, was burnt to the ground and most of the city was destroyed, an event which sent shock-waves of terror - graphically described in contemporary chronicles - through the Carolingian world.

Ten years later Nantes was sacked again and nearly a century would elapse before the Viking menace was past and Alain Barbetorte, a count of Nantes and first to call himself duke of Brittany, revitalised the city and made it his capital. The Musée Dobrée holds some exceptional Viking relics, including seven swords salvaged from the river bed in almost perfect condition.

The current cathedral took getting on for five hundred years to complete from its inception by Duke Jean V in 1434. The façade of this deeply attractive building is in the long process of being cleaned. Now gleaming sections of Loire limestone on the west face are echoed by a luminous whiteness within, the marble floor dappled with coloured squares of light reflected from the fine windows. A woman on her knees in a side chapel is reading from a book, mouthing the words silently to the saint, a stuffed shopping bag on the floor beside her. I wonder if this is her routine - shop first then pray, or was it a sudden urge this morning to seek spiritual comfort?

The tomb of François II and his second wife Marguerite de Foix, parents of Anne de Bretagne, was moved to the cathedral early in the 19th century after being shifted from its original siting in the Chapelle des Carmes during revolutionary upheavals. Stately marble figures of the Four cardinal virutes man the corners, the most striking being the curiously double-headed Prudence. Presumably this sculptural motif derives from the iconography of Janus, but it will come as no surprise to afficianados of the Harry Potter films. Historians in centuries to come may pick up and make who knows what of that connection.

The hotel where I'm staying is staffed by cheerful, friendly youngsters. I spend a lot of time in the lobby (using the guest computer as my own refuses stubbornly to connect to the internet) and admire their well-judged responses to a wide variety of guests. I hope their bosses recognise what an asset these bright young women are. The hotel, with its sleek lines of modernist décor and open, easy atmosphere fuelled by a sense of natural energy, seems an epitome of Nantes, a smart-casual metaphor for the early 21st century.

There's no restaurant here, only a small breakfast room, but a supper tray of soup, cheese and fruit can be collected from reception and carried precariously up to your room in the tiny lift. Having walked many miles of pavements, I choose this welcome option despite the rare and always pleasurable possibility of strolling at night in city streets. Besides, my head is throbbing from bombardment of images and information I've absorbed. On television is a strange film where knights in pseudo-medieval armour are mutilating each other in a Dark Age landscape. The all-pervading mist from which they emerge and recede seems an apt metaphor for the director's foggy grasp of history. I wouldn't mind this if the story was compelling, but after half an hour I have no idea of the plot if there is one. They are men of few words, these phantoms of confused chronology, but they make my head worse and silent darkness comes as a great relief.

The Nantes-Brest canal was conceived as a means of linking the arsenals of those two cities by an inland route, to avoid the predatory English fleets so consistently harassing and blockading the Breton coast in the second part of the 18th century. In the aftermath of the War of the Austrian succession the French fleet had suffered a disastrous defeat in the Atlantic off Brest, and again in the 1780s fall-out from the American War of Independence brought English ships to menace the ports of Brittany. The need for an internal supply line to maintain traffic between Nantes, Brest and Lorient became increasingly urgent and there were obvious industrial and commercial advantages to linkage between the main ports, especially when Rennes and St-Malo were also connected to the chain by a north-south waterway, using the Vilaine and the Rance. After various proposals, a commission finally began serious investigation in 1783 and their findings were presented to the king, Louis XVI. The Revolution put matters in abeyance, but in 1804 Napoleon authorised the project. Work began in Nantes in 1810, but little trace of those original efforts remains today.

Early in the morning with a cool sun low in the sky, I make my way from the hotel down towards the Loire, passing the landmark of the lavishly decorative LU tower. Here Nantes' most famous product, LU biscuits - and in particular the Petit Beurre - were manufactured for many years from the mid-19th century by the Lefèvre-Utile family business, from ingredients plentifully imported from the Caribbean. The huge success of the business was a triumph of marketing as well as product, with clever use of slogans and contemporary art - such as art nouveau metal boxes - to promote a wide range of biscuits developed by the company. There were 300 employees in 1889, and over a thousand twenty-five years later, generating more than 6000 tons of biscuits each year. Production moved out of the city in the 1980s, but the biscuits are still ubiquitous today, with LU sadly a brand-name of the multi-national giant Danone.

That identity is closely tied with marketing is a given of the modern world. A well-projected name or slogan insinuates itself into the mind and acts as a powerful trigger of association that impels our hand to reach for a particular packet on the supermarket shelf or place a cross in one box before all others. Labels are powerful tools of identity, but they have their dangers in the human sphere. Giving oneself a label is often part of the process of projecting our own image, making it easier for others to assimilate and understand how we wish to be seen. People joining political parties or social groups are often establishing an alibi of identity for themselves in the process. The problem lies in the assumptions that follow, often in direct denial of the complexities of individual identity. Everyone relating to that generic term - Tory, Christian, Irish, teacher, cyclist, etc. - is automatically lumped together in a massively simplistic judgment. I had already noticed this tendency within my own family before I was ten, already feeling the painful conflict of a sense of separateness and at the same time a longing to be part of a group. In our household labels were put on people to make it easy to condemn them. If someone voted the wrong way or spoke with a certain accent they were not worth bothering with. A relation once maintained in an argument that farmers were not good people and could not be so - how very much easier it is to assimilate and dismiss people en masse rather than face the complexities of individualism and life outside the box!

Beyond the Lu tower, I come out by the water of the Erdre. This river, initial link in the chain of canalised rivers across Brittany, flows into the Loire just south of the ancient city centre. The large modern mechanised maritime Lock St-Félix today is technically the first of the Nantes-Brest canal, but the Erdre then runs freely northward for 20 kilometres before the canal proper turns off westward at Quiheix.

The course of this river within Nantes changed significantly during the 1930s: the original route was filled in and is now a major road - Cours des 50 Otages, a reference to Nazi reprisals for the death of one of their officers. Karl Holtz had been involved as an engineer on the tunnel housing the Erdre, built as part of the German war reparations programme, before returning to Nantes in WWII as a Feld Kommandant, only to be assassinated by a resistance fighter in 1941.

The original first lock of the canal at this eastern end, constructed in 1828, was nick-named Ecluse de Madame, after the foundation stone was laid by the Duchess of Berry. When that ambitious lady fell from political grace by virtue of plotting to put her Bourbon son Louis on the throne of a restored monarchy in the 1830s, the name was no longer used, and the lock itself was later lost under the new road in the city's redevelopment. The first boat on the canal left Nantes on June 19th 1834 with a cargo of iron bound for St-Malo, and huge crowds came out in the rain to celebrate this historic departure.

Today the short stretch of water from Ecluse St-Félix up to the tunnel that takes the Erdre underground also carries the name of the saint, who was bishop of Nantes for more than thirty years in the second half of the 6th century and exerted great influence on the development of the city in more than spiritual ways, devising plans for improving navigation around the nascent settlement by flooding the surrounding marshes.

The tunnel of the Erdre runs for half a kilometre, passing close to the ducal chateau and the cathedral before emerging near the Pont St-Mihiel. I cannot resist taking a navette bus for this meagre distance. There are no other passengers and the charming man who hands over my ticket encourages me to go outside at the back to get the best atmosphere on the very short journey. The boat seems to move at a fair speed, water churning behind, slopping from side to side under the low arched ceiling. The channel curves and light behind disappears, but we are suddenly out into the bright sunshine again by the Quai de Versailles. I walk along to the bridge and look up river. Boats, one a crêperie, many substantial residences, are moored on either side. The channel of the Erdre stretches enticingly northwards. This begins to feel like the start of a journey.

There is no towpath by which to follow the river's course - the proposal of 1811 for this never found favour - so boats had to be pulled by tugs or rely on sail at the start of their journey to the canal proper. Only certain stretches of the banks of the Erdre are accessible to walkers today because of private property development along the river, so I content myself with strolling along the urban section, attractive enough around the Ile de Versailles, with its elaborate and watery Japanese garden.

I have walked many miles around Nantes in the last few days, city walking - hard on the ankles, stopping, starting, swerving and standing all contributing to a stiffness in the legs that is commoner with age. I can't wait to get going properly, to tread a continuous path and loosen up every limb and muscle.

Physically I'm ready, but a certain psychological apprehension lurks beneath the surface of my optimism about this adventure. It's not a rocky or uneven path that's going to be hazardous, but the long thought that will catch me out. The theme of identity which is to develop into a major aspect of this book strikes right at the beginning of the thought processes about my journey. Walking the canal with all its varied scenery is also to prove a means of exploring an inner landscape.

Chapter 2   The Marches of Brittany

"Walks are the unobtrusive connecting thread of other memories,
and yet each walk is a little drama itself"
Leslie Stephen

Starting this section of the journey at Lock No. 2 where the canal proper leaves the Erdre poses a problem. Access to such a symbolically significant spot apparently requires hitting the canal 2kms up at a bridge, walking back to the lock and then retracing one's steps, which rather spoils that 'setting out' feeling. This rigmarole creates something of an anti-climax for a moment I've looked forward to for a long time.

Ecluse Quiheix is a pretty lock, green-painted and decorated with red geraniums, a simplicity unfortunately lacking further along the line. A few metres beyond to the east lies the surprisingly broad estuary of the Erdre, from which the canal slips off quietly, tracing its way westward like an opaque finger. The long straight stretch of towpath back from the lock is busy with joggers and cyclists and a roller-skater stylishly kitted out in black, travelling at great speed. Once past the little bridge again I feel I'm on the way and walk for an hour or more without seeing another person.

Solitude and the separation from society, from one's normal life, are common motives for walking: the soothing presence of the landscape and the gentle physical rhythm are restorative. I'm in need of space and peace at the moment, but on a walk of this length it's impossible to avoid issues without the carpet of daily living to sweep them under. Falling seems to be the theme of this early part of my day metaphorically in a momentary sinking of spirits and literally - acorns fall from the oaks and plop into the canal, apples thud from mistletoe-bound branches onto the towpath and prickly bright green horse chestnuts bounce and skitter in front of me. It takes longer than usual to settle into a physical rhythm. Carrying such a heavy pack changes my stride pattern and takes some adjustment in the alignment of my body. I soon feel myself distorting into an S-shape and try to stay upright. After a half-an-hour or so, I'm walking fluidly at last.

It's very hot with the sun on my back, although autumnal storms are forecast later. The water looks thick, green and surprisingly dirty. Several times today I walk through a patch of hot, damp sewery smell, which puts all thoughts of swimming very far from my mind. Soon I see a black bag floating in the water, bicycle inner-tube hanging out and who knows what else within - incredibly, in all my years of waterside walking in Brittany, this is the first time I've seen rubbish like that. But this section of the canal certainly leaves a lot to be desired in terms of water quality, as I am to find out later.

The land is fairly flat and rather noisy with roads nearby, so cars and lorries compete in cacophony with farm machinery, lowing cattle and the raucous shout of greedy crows. Little boats line the banks as if locals use the water routinely, and it is certainly true that the canal is much more peopled here in the east of Brittany - I am to see more cyclists, joggers, walkers and fishermen than anywhere else on this walk, over 300kms away from the end in Finistère.

Coming up the slope to the next lock, La Tindière, I'm jolted from some wishful thoughts by a tiny red squirrel dancing across the path right in front of me before leaping into an ivy-covered tree. This is a common pattern, being jerked back to the present and immediate by a reminder from nature that I'm in her kingdom and owe her fealty.

The lock-house here reflects the standard issue to come. Regulation bright green paint - a colour nature has wisely left alone - and a bland large white board giving the name and number of the lock and distances to the next and last one. Utilitarian, ugly. But Loire-Atlantique is to prove a startlingly unaesthetic place in many ways. (By the time I reach Lock 16 the inhabitant has removed the hideous white board to the side of an outhouse well away from the lock, a great improvement for his living environment.)

The idea of getting somewhere is inherent in any journey. There's an element of the unpredictable in this trip, although I have places to stay arranged. How my timing or stamina will be, I have no idea. To travel for days without a watch is interesting. At last I'm doing what I've wanted to since first thinking of writing this book - walking the canal from an unknown beginning. The sense of exploration and stimulation is suddenly exhilarating. Even though the territory is hardly attractive, I feel alive and sensorily receptive to colours and smells fermented by the heat of the sun. The sounds are still mainly limited to intrusive traffic noise from the road bridge at Pont du Plessis, but at least this also heralds the first pretty stretch of the day, a sweeping bend lined by graceful tall trees. This is a relief, as my impression so far is certainly nothing special.

The landscape is dull and predictable as so often where the terrain is worked and managed. Farms appear on both sides, with their herds grazing in the lush fields. It's a workaday stretch of canal, that's for sure, suddenly brightened by a fruit farm on the opposite bank with scarecrows dressed in plastic raincoats - one in a white-hooded cape moves like a lively ghost.

This linking section (*bief de partage*) of the canal at Bout-de-Bois joining the Erdre and the Isac is fed by the *rigole de Vioreau* which brought water from 22kms away via four aqueducts and a 600m underground section. It was built by more than a thousand Spanish prisoners from the Napoleonic Wars of the early 19th century. They were housed in wooden barracks where the river Isac now meets the canal, in the commune of Saffré. By the time I reach the site of the camp, the rain is torrential and I have to abandon all thoughts of exploring and paying respects to these poor men, but it's hard not to dwell on their grim struggle with physical toil in appalling conditions. Apparently those that dropped dead were buried where they lay, so I may well be walking over bones right now. The more fortunate few were able to return to Spain after the fall of the Empire.

Originally the canal project was well-received as a source of employment for local people across Brittany, but that changed when the low wages and appalling conditions of labour became apparent. It was then necessary to use free workers from other parts of France like the Limousin and the Auvergne where work was scarce, as well as bringing in prisoners of war and deserters who had no choice in the matter and whose suffering was a matter of indifference to the local communities.

In complete contrast to this pathetic plight of human history, there are a lot of self-satisfied notices along the route proclaiming all that is currently being done in the name of *aménagement* ('development') of the canal. This is a word I am coming to hate and the reality here is horrible. Noisy little aquatic diggers buzz back and forth across the water lifting huge mechanical armfuls of weed and depositing them on the bank to be collected by lorries with huge mechanical arms. Trees are being hacked down along stretches of the towpath: official boards assure us that they are past it (not by the look of many solid severed trunks) and hold out the dizzy promise of replanting - all I see in that context are some young firs, hardly a fitting substitute for the glory of deciduous growth.

And it gets worse. The *halte nautique* is a perfectly sensible concept - a place for boaters, walkers and cyclists to stop under shelter, read information boards, use the toilets, etc. But the realisation here in Loire Atlantique defies belief in its hideousness - toy-town urinal meets twee Swiss cottage is a charitable description. What is the matter with the powers that be that they cannot produce something natural and unobtrusive in the way of 'canal furniture'? Have they never heard the word simplicity? Yes, facilities are needed, but a single toilet in a stupidly elaborate chalet placed right on the towpath is a triumph of misconception and philistinism. On the other hand, I see not one SINGLE seat (apart from picnic tables at road junctions) along the whole length of the canal in several days of walking. What about some rough wooden benches or even the regular slabs of concrete in Finistère which provide somewhere to sit down? Why not have a go at providing something that those who use the canal actually need? Maybe the designers and planners have limited experience of the reality they are supposed to cater for, or perhaps there's just a lack of passion or sensibility for the environment in this context.

Fortunately a waterside proprietor has placed a couple of rickety seats on the track leading to his NO ENTRY signs, a concession of largesse, so one can sit off the towpath in shade, but not penetrate his privacy. As there is a lull in the rain, I stop here to have lunch, although there's no doubt that storm clouds are on the horizon. There are quite a few inside my head by now too.

The first claps of thunder begin as soon as I resume my walk. Away to the left an increasingly lowering sky promises the expected storm. As the light goes down, the canal looks different, less banal, more interesting in a mean and moody fashion. The rain begins to spatter and I'm forced to put on the startling blue plastic poncho I have purchased for just this eventuality. A herd of black and white cows (will I ever be able to tell a pie noir from a Friesian?) stare mindlessly at this bizarre apparition tramping along the towpath, emitting the odd Anglo-Saxon swear word as the torrent increases and there is no prospect of shelter.

Even the excessively flowery locks with their brash madness are beginning to annoy me. It's that sort of day. They seem to be vying with each other to produce the most unnatural looking setting - pampas grass in vast quantities is probably the winner, but the strident red-hot-pokers are almost as bad as the electric storm for giving me another thumping headache. Does no-one in Loire-Atlantique include the word 'natural' in their vocabulary either?

At the bridge at Les Coudrais the towpath moves to the south bank of the canal. Here it is raised high above the water, with another tier of grass verge below. Opposite, the rough track runs just above the canal so this whole long stretch has a strange lop-sided feel, appropriate to my own perceptions as lightning flashes all around me and thunder breaks directly overhead. I cannot risk the tape or camera getting soaked, so put them away and trudge on in bitter mood. Water is the element governing the emotions, and I can certainly feel it acting up in me today, as I kick savagely at fallen apples on the towpath. This is a fine place for long thoughts, but what stays with me is the incredible toil and effort of cutting this artificial section through the terrain - I can almost hear the straining, cracking joints of men bent double under loads of earth and stones. In following any path one is to some extent simply validating the route (or its construction in this case) of those now long absent.

How much more rain can fall? A thunderous deluge thumps down onto the canal and lightning repeatedly streaks across the sky behind me. I can't help but remember Thierry Guidet's excellent, laconic account of his walk along this same canal fifteen years ago, especially his comment on this particular stretch: *je suis entré au royaume de l'eau*. He was referring to the canal, the rivers and the marshes that lie all around and into whose water-retentive earth each footstep sinks. I share his feeling today, but in this case, the water is coming downwards.

A brief respite is offered by another *halte nautique* - am I prepared to sacrifice my aesthetic principles? You bet I am. There is nowhere to sit in this one (an odd omission even by Loire-Atlantique standards) so I hang my saturated poncho from a jutting beam and sink down on a wooden step. I am soon joined by a cheerful woman from the boat moored alongside, who is curious about what I'm doing, and then insists on writing down my name and website address so she can look out for the book next year. She's a Breton, but left to escape the negative energies of granite - not the first time I've heard this story - and is now happily dry in the Drôme for most of the year, apart from a regular soggy sojourn on this northern canal. She deplores the vandalism evident along the canal route and I tell her it is uncommon further west. We have a good talk and I feel a slight pang as I wave the boat off. One of the men shrugs sympathetically and calls '*bon courage*' as they drift back towards Nort-sur-Erdre.

My eventual arrival at La Chevellerais epitomizes a wet

Monday afternoon in rural France. Everything is shut and the atmosphere is depressingly dead. As I try to summon the last reserves of my energy for a 2 kilometre trek to the only guesthouse for miles around, I am constantly showered and spattered with water by drivers passing unnecessarily close - within inches in one case - on a long empty road. I hate walking away from the canal and it becomes an excruciating endurance test, but at least there is a degree of amused sympathy and, more importantly, a pot of hot coffee when I finally stagger in.

The same downpour opens its arms to receive me as I leave early in the morning. I cannot help reflecting, uncharitably maybe, that nine out of ten English B&B owners would have offered to run me back to the canal. As it is I arrive there forty minutes later, already soaked and forced to seek refuge for an hour in the hideous *halte nautique*. As I passed through the village, an apparently normal woman stared at me round-eyed: my appearance has clearly made the leap from the ridiculous to downright scary overnight. I am glad to be leaving La Chevellerais.

The canal now has very much the look of Kipling's 'great grey-green, greasy Limpopo river, all set about with fever trees', but at least for a short while it is a quieter section, with the more enclosed and self-contained atmosphere so familiar to me from canal walking in western Brittany.

I am beginning to get the measure geographically of these borderlands, fought over by the Franks and Bretons from the 6th century and later ravaged by the Vikings. Here Waroc harried and chivvied the Franks in the 580s, advancing and retreating, making peace expediently only in order to regroup for renewed warfare. His efforts were followed up by Judicael before some degree of *rapprochement* with king Dagobert in a treaty forged near Paris. Those were the glory days of Breton history, passionate resistance against the encroaching menace of outsiders, a refusal to be pushed back to the watery limits of the peninsula, a full-blooded determination to assert worth and identity.

Emperors of the Franks Pépin the Short and then Charlemagne characteristically took more robust measures to protect the western edge of their vast empire, establishing this buffer zone of the Marches of Brittany, roughly in the triangle of Nantes, Vannes and Rennes, under the control of nominees he could rely on. According to the Chanson de Roland, which I am re-reading on this trip, the great warrior hero himself was Count of the Marches, a Frankish overlord protecting the interests of Charlemagne on the flat wet borders of Brittany. Roland must have got quite a shock when he saw the high arid mountain peaks of the Pyrenees en route to his bizarre death at the pass of Roncevaux in 778.

Here where identity was fought over for many hundreds of years, I'm thinking again about my Welsh/English problem. Last week at the market in Morlaix, an elderly Breton stops to tell me, seriously and vindictively, I should not be selling books in English and furthermore the English should get out, or be chucked out, of Brittany. It is not pleasant to be faced by such blind prejudice (for the first time) and my colleague Christian on the next stall gallantly intervenes, eventually leading the man away and continuing the argument with him. Five minutes later, he tells me gleefully that apparently I am responsible for the death of Jeanne d'Arc. This cheers up all the traders enormously on what had been a slow day and leads to serial jokes along the lines of - don't ask her, she'll have you burnt at the stake, and, how could you do such a horrible thing to poor Jeanne (well, she deserved it and I did warn her). I've been thinking of having a sign made to read, in French: I AM WELSH. PLEASE DON'T HOLD ME RESPONSIBLE FOR THE ENGLISH.

It is so easy to succumb to the comfort of the label, to cling to the skirts of a protective concept. I'm pursuing my path here like thousands of other Britons staking their current claim to Breton soil but this national distinction seems important to me. To be fair to myself, I have always answered (with feeling) Welsh in situations where the nationality question has been posed. It is not a 'Celtic' affectation brought on by moving to Brittany, but here the issue seems raw and personal. Perhaps it is easier just to accept the rootless, stateless identity that has seemed my lot in life up until recently, a citizen of the earth at best. But if so, how can I feel this degree of passionate attachment to Finistère, this umbilical cord of connection to the land beneath my feet as I tramp the Monts d'Arrée and measure the old tracks of wolves in the Landes de Cragou?

The canal is now skirting the edge of the Forêt de la Groulais, a slight steam rising from the surface of the water as there is a pause in the rain and the temperature rises. After Lock 11, La Prée, the canal opens out and a tarmac road leads all the way up to Blain. This is hard on the feet and creates an unwelcoming expectation of vehicular traffic at any moment. It engenders the sense that one is not in a natural environment, one's rightful place, and a degree of competition with other modes of transport is introduced. At least I can strip the dreadful poncho off and walk freely again.

A flowery passerelle provides the crossing point to the château of Blain. This fine-looking structure, dating from 1104, was once home to the Clisson family before the Rohans - subject of a later chapter - got their hands on it and fashioned a centre of Protestant resistance under Henri de Rohan in the Wars of Religion or '*les guerres de Monsieur de Rohan*'. The sumptuous logis du Roi was added later: its vaulted roof is supposed to be exceptional.

Blain was once the capital of the Namnètes tribe and then an important centre of the Roman communications network. After spinning out two hours in the now unremarkable town over lunch-time, I trudge back out to the château eagerly. It's incredibly impressive at close range, and I'm keen to explore. Except it's closed. I use the mobile phone to call and get a recorded message. I phone the Tourist Office, which expresses surprise and ignorance. They agree with me that it should be open but it doesn't seem an issue of any significance in their book.

Now I really am spitting mad. It's raining hard, I'm weary and apparently face the prospect of an afternoon in this ghastly place without access to the monument that was my reason for stopping here in the first place. I look around for someone to beg to let me in, but apart from three youths strimming grass in the moat (and wearing head-sets) ready for the medieval fête, there is no-one. I trail back to the canal and sink down on a bench in the rain. Six donkeys come over at once for a chat and we chew things over for a while without any firm conclusions, but from their squirming in mud and throwing their legs in the air I sense a general sympathy with my own frustration. The only light relief is a study of Blain's street map - rue Wootton Bassett (another ghastly place) makes me laugh out loud, and the joke of *allée Nominoë* leading into *impasse Erispoë*, neatly encapsulating the frustrations of Breton kingship in the 9th century, does something to raise my spirits.

Finally I give up pretending to enjoy myself, buy some food and head for my accommodation. The owner is charming and insists on plying me with large amounts of sangria left over from a family lunch. We have an interesting chat in which she expresses a dislike for people from Morbihan and a preference for those from Finistère. I'm OK, having the magical 02 98 phone number. When I finally totter up the stairs, there is an exceedingly fine line between my exhaustion and drunkenness. It is only as I fall into bed that I notice an entire horde of mosquitoes in the room, just biding their time. A terrible night ensues as they toy mercilessly with me, making sure to buzz me awake each time before inflicting their bloody wounds. The incredible noise of traffic on the main road outside punctuates my struggles with the insect world throughout the night.

I survive, and emerge in the morning, blurry-eyed and itching all over. Goodbye Blain. From now on things can only improve and, despite the weather, they do.

Chapter 3   Life after Blain

"I stroll along serenely, with my eyes, my shoes, my rage,
forgetting everything"
Pablo Neruda

Away from Blain, for the first time bird song takes precedence over mechanical noise. Green fields and gentle slopes are peaceful in the light mist of morning, whilst across the water it's wilder, with trees pressing right down to the canal. Fishermen are out in force, but unusually for the breed - and this is a ludicrous plus for Loire-Atlantique - every single one greets me in a friendly manner. Some even want to talk: must be a slow day, even by fishy standards.

There's a large, well-fenced establishment on the opposite bank which I immediately take for some sort of military set-up, although the location seems odd, but a later look at the map indicates a vast psychiatric hospital. The car-park seems to have the best view of this idyllic setting.

There's been an orgy of tree-felling along this bank, but the aftermath, a careless mess of mangled trunks and branches, remains un-cleared as if the purpose is in the destruction, and once this highest peak of excitement has been reached, the energy of completion is scattered and lost. What look like water-rats are splashing in the pondweed-covered stagnant pools to the right of the towpath, where they have little competition for a settled habitat. On the other side, the canal is now opening out into a broad and welcoming river.

It's taken 5kms this morning to walk the heaviness out of my legs and get into a comfortable physical state after such a bad night. Now on a very quiet stretch, I'm starting to relax and my mind takes over, leaving the body just doing its job.

A man with his dog who passed me at a jogging pace right back in Blain is now on his way back and stops to ask about where I'm going. We enjoy the sort of friendly pointless exchange that leaves each participant with the sense that he has briefly brightened someone else's life, whereas the reverse is usually the case. Shortly after, I cross a small road to lie on the wet seat of a picnic table and a fishermen gets up from the bank to follow me and advise me on the importance of having a good rest. Some instinct tells me not to prolong this particular conversation, but people are certainly very talkative today!

Before each of the next two locks, the river opens out even further into the shape of small lakes. The Pont de Barel is overshadowed by the noise and dust of a working quarry on the far bank, and its dirty lorries going to and fro thunder recklessly over a very narrow bridge. At Lock No.14 (Barelle), the lock-house is empty, but a lock-keeper emerges from a little office hut to start winding the lock-gate open as a large boat flying a Union Jack is approaching. I stay to watch them through the lock, three cheerful couples who handle the manoeuvre competently. They tell me they are experienced canal-users, but have never seen a filthier canal than this one. Apparently the boats have no holding-tanks and empty sewage directly into the water. Can this really be true? They seem genuinely shocked by the state of the canal. I get the same impression of the water quality from other sailors along this stretch and it's only confirmation of my own observation and olfactory nerve.

This party hired their boat in Nort-sur-Erdre and have been up as far as Guenrouet, where I'm headed today. With a practised routine, they're through the lock incredibly quickly and off again. The 'captain' is enjoying himself as if starring in a boy's adventure story and wants to put his special hat on for my photograph.

There is a certain degree of stoicism inherent in a long, slow journey, a resignation to the fact that eventually one will arrive without necessarily knowing when or even how. But there is a marked tendency to give oneself spatial references to mark passage and progress: how many times do I find myself saying into the tape-recorder, 'approaching a road bridge,' or 'another lock coming up'. Similarly I went through a phase of photographing every kilometre stone in my early days of canal walking, when this acknowledgement and connection seemed crucially important and a bizarre form of respect.

The stretch I'm passing along must house a heronry: it's common here to see more than one bird at a time, gliding untroubled and silent from bank to bank and water to tree. How infinitely civilized their presence feels after the company of crows. One of the many benefits of long distance walking is the luxury of extended observation, which lends an added awareness of distinctive characters within the world of animals and plants.

Around La Touche aux Thebauds, a sense of domesticity falls on the canal, as houses with dining terraces looking down on the water proliferate and a line of makeshift bridges link their gardens to the towpath. At Lock 15, La Touche, a French family are bringing their boat through the unmanned lock with a little gentle grumbling between the generations. It has to be said that those on boats seem genuinely relaxed, enjoying the benefits of an undemanding holiday amid unfurling scenery, where the greatest challenge is to throw a loop of rope over a mooring-stone.

With the D3 at Pont Nozay behind me, I cannot wait any longer for a seat and despite the wet grass, sink down at the foot of a large knobbly pine tree. I can smell the sap already tracing its receding autumnal path to earth. Eating some disgusting remains of squashed sandwich, I am entertained by a display of acrobatics from several red squirrels on the opposite bank. They are having enormous fun, leaping and gamboling from branch to branch, tree to tree so the hillside seems alive with shivering leaves. Sitting still like this, especially at ground level, makes one part of the landscape, able to participate passively in the feast of nature.

I believe, being an optimist by nature, that the weather has finished tormenting me: today has been overcast, with a little sunshine here, a few drops of rain there, but quite manageable and conducive to walking. Luckily I have no idea of what is actually in store.

The marshy nature of the land is more and more apparent north-west towards Guenrouet, with *marais* to the right and water meadows little above the level of the canal on the other side. The atmosphere is quiet, absorbent, with only the measured sound of my tread, heavy under the weight of the pack.

A series of lovely looping bends heralds the approach to my destination and for the first time the scenery becomes a positive feature of the canal's setting. The long view to the left towards St-Gildas-de-Bois is beautiful. On this side, metal meshing reinforces the stability of the steep banks where the Château de Carheil lies on a densely wooded hill, only its walls and a tiny chapel visible from the towpath. A surly young man is fishing next to the NO FISHING sign: it's good to have my lack of faith in fishermen restored after a brief honeymoon period today. Somewhere high on the hill a guard dog hears me and gives a series of deep resonant barks that echo all around. I notice a greasy oil-slick on the surface of an inlet and the general filthiness of the water again.

The wide river narrows to the road bridge at Guenrouet. I sit at a wooden picnic table to catch my breath and take in an attractive scene; the camp site opposite (where I shall be staying), the spire of the church on its green hill, boats happily plying the channel. The church at Guenrouet, visually impressively dominant, has an interesting past, reflecting like many others the vicissitudes of Breton history. This was the site of a religious foundation as early as the 11th century, an edifice enlarged and transformed over the centuries until it met the common revolutionary fate of serving as a stables, whilst the bells were taken to Savenay to be melted down for coin. In 1793, the local priest, Guillaume Legrand, was taken from his prison and drowned at Nantes, one of many to die for their beliefs in the grim waters of the Loire.

With the 19th century revival of religion, a new church was constructed in the 1890s, although the 55m bell tower was not finished until 1910. This was placed, unusually for the time, on the west face, apparently at the behest of the maire whose motive was based on his residence, the handsome building still adjoining the church today.

As the Allies fought to liberate Brittany in 1944, this line of territory along the canal here marked the boundary between the Germans still firmly entrenched in St-Nazaire and the Americans, who bombarded the villages along the valleys over many months. The church at Guenrouet was a particular target, as it was thought that the Germans were using it as a look-out - from the elevation, it's hard to imagine they weren't. On December 7 1944, the bell-tower was finally shelled into oblivion, and the population of Guenrouet evacuated soon after.

The church was eventually restored, with a series of stained-glass windows by Gabriel Loire from Chartres adorning the interior, under the device *diruta restitui*.

I cross the bridge and trek up to the campsite. An efficient young woman greets me, takes my money and, as the first ominous claps of thunder break overhead, leads me swiftly to a caravan with a large side awning creating an extra covered area. When she has departed and a sheet of rain is noisily pounding the metal structure, I have plenty of time to realize that I have just paid 32 euros for a 'room' without water (except leaks), heating, toilet or sheets. And there is apparently no food available on site, despite advertising to the contrary. I'm desperately hungry and almost equally keen to discover the pleasures of the 'facilities block'. As I get up to look out of the window, the table collapses and drops its full weight across my left leg just above the knee, causing me to yell with pain. No-one could hear in the racket of the storm. One glance out of the window reveals that what was recently a neat tarmac path wending its way down through the site towards the canal is now a river in its own right. The sky is dramatically dark, which shows off the savage lightning to better effect. There is nothing for it but adopt a siege mentality and read the Chanson de Roland.

An hour later my ear is quick to pick up a lull in the rain and I weigh up my options carefully. Wet boots stare coldly up at me from the mat and I decide to make a quick dash outside in the only other pair of shoes I have with me. The path is wet, but not running with water and I'm perfectly happy with my decision until washing my hands in a tiled cubicle, trying not to look in a mirror of alarming clarity. It's then that the insistent drum-beat of rain strikes the roof with a manic intensity. Outside, the path is a river again within seconds. I wade back uphill, water over my ankles, shoes probably ruined. Back to the bloody pass at Roncevaux, where Roland is spurring his horse about manfully and splitting skulls with gusto.

The rain really has stopped now. I put my wet boots back on and slog up to the village half a kilometre away to buy food and have a much-needed coffee in the bar. The woman in the delicatessen refuses to let me look around while she serves the next customer. I appeal to him but he is clearly more scared of her than me. Madame constantly questions and chivies me as I end up buying a crazy selection of items I don't want. When I come out, it's raining again, but the church is open and I get to see the lurid but curiously effective stained glass that is the local pride.

By the time I'm ensconced, shivering, in the dreadful caravan again it feels as if everything I possess is soaking. Luckily I've remembered to buy a newspaper to stuff in my boots to have a hope of drying them by morning. I really do appreciate the fine efforts of the journalists whose work serves such a practical purpose in the world. I eat the dreary cold food mechanically without tasting anything, but retain just enough wit to dive aside as the table collapses a second time. The storm outside is violent and relentless, raging directly overhead for the best part of two hours.

I'm cold and weary. Roland has burst his blood vessels blowing Oliphant to call for aid against the treachery of Ganelon. The more I think about it, the more shockingly careless and unheroic his death seems. In medieval Scotland they would probably have put the horn on trial rather than honouring it as Charlemagne did. Memories of wet childhood holidays in caravans in South Wales force Roland aside and loom like spectres in the dank atmosphere. If there is anything on earth more depressing than being stuck in a metal box with rain rattling all around, it's thinking about my family. Before nine o'clock, I wrap myself in a green blanket, curl up on the mattress and fall deeply asleep. For eleven hours.

The last day of my trip is virtually rain-free. I retain surprisingly positive memories of Guenrouet with its pretty port, wooded river banks and impressive church. The latter's bell chimes with richly sonorous voice as I leave for the last stage up to Redon. It's cool and pleasant for walking along the glassy and gracious Isac on a slightly misty morning. Cattle sitting grazing lazily in the fields remind me of Charlemagne's horses, exhausted after the great battle of revenge: *'if they want grass, they crop it as they lie / He that has suffered learns many things in life'*. The spire of Guenrouet remains visible behind for many a long kilometre.

Unlike the previous few days, most of today's walking consists of long, straight stretches. The towpath of orange gravel, kindly giving to the feet, is banked up like a causeway between the canal and the marshes which drift away on both sides. The Isac is at its widest here: grey clouds racing overhead skim in reflection over the rippling surface. Dotted along the route are rough cabins between the towpath and the serious marsh: providing shelter for fishermen, these mostly have tin roofs on top and rough benches within and they are imbued with the moisture of the spongy earth below.

The simplicity of canal walking and its relatively narrow physical scope makes the switch to inner focus all too easy, with emotional floodlights tending to swamp this quiet stage when the green enclosure holds thought on a single track. The constant company of water, so closely tied to the emotions, is another encouraging factor. One effect of long-distance walking is to emphasise the suitability of a gentle measured pace to both reflection and observation, lending time for musings to mix and settle into new patterns. Sometimes the canal seems to perform the function of the gallery in 16th century castles, which provided exercise without distraction before the development of gardens and the wilder attractions of nature rose to the fore. Contemporary Breton travel-writer Jean-Claude Bourlès was bored by this lack of surprise along the canal. He describes throwing pebbles into the water for the pleasure of creating change. Despite the boon of seeing otters, he finds the silence and omnipresence of nature *trop lourd*. I suppose that monotony must be in the eye of the beholder.

I suddenly enter a little concentration of fishermen, and a multitude of smiling greetings. Even a man fishing from a little boat in the middle of the river on a wide bend nods courteously in my direction. It's like receiving a benediction: I feel as welcome as a shoal of salmon. Four swans graciously nod regally in my direction too - truly a day of fitting in, at last. I don't feel the need to scratch that old scab of identity quite so roughly.

The walking soon gets lonely again. I'm virtually on a spit amid the canal and the vast, stagnant marshes. There is nothing between me and saturation save for a couple of feet of orange gravel. Large chunks of rock are needed to baulk up the sides of the path and stop the whole thing slipping away into the kingdom of the *marais*. The size of the river is overwhelming and, as the sun comes out, even more lovely, as an odd configuration of large trees on both sides of the towpath creates an unexpected avenue of verdure.

I pass the 79 kilometre stone, hoping for a rest but gradually giving up my fantasies of a seat before Redon. This lack must reflect a dearth of recreational walking in this area or a local authority that spends far too much time sitting down - although in fact, I should welcome this element of hardship in what is after all a form of pilgrimage. My homage to the canal positively requires this physical effort, intermittent pain of one sort or another and necessary commitment to get to the end to elevate the journey into something special. I don't see how that same effect can be achieved by bike (too swift) or boat (too easy). This section of the walk has been a bit of an endurance test at times, and not just physically, but nothing will stop me finishing it now. Only 12 kilometres to go.

The Isac divides from the canal in an area of attractive low-hilled countryside, the variety of contours embracing the soft, wide river as it braves its way through the marsh that constantly threatens to tie it down. It's not long before the orphaned canal is dusty and dirty again. Approaching the bridge at Pont Miny, a crayfish scurries across the path in front of me and then stops, raising a claw in challenge or defence. I cross the canal by the garish (pink and dark blue) Maison du Canal which appears to be shut up, and sit for an hour in the picnic area, reading the Song of Roland and eating whatever bits of food I can find lurking in my bag. I long for an orange or some carrots, having had more than enough of carbohydrates and dubious protein on this trip. On the other hand, my first hot meal in four days will be something to look forward to.

From here the wind gets up, as I start the long haul up to the last lock before Redon. White cattle from a huge farm are spread over the hills and fields, enjoying these lush grazing grounds. I walk into a cloud of yellow and blue butterflies, who are happy to dance attendance on me for a few metres to the extent that I feel deliberately escorted.

The canal, the colour of ash, is quite narrow here, starved of sustenance from the Isac, which continues to flow a field away. The atmosphere is suddenly close and heavy, and when the sun forces its way out of its prison of grey clouds the heat on the back of my head is intense and not pleasant. I'm gradually becoming aware of a nasty pain on the skin on one side of my neck. I have no mirror with me to check the symptoms, and there's nothing to be done about it anyway, but I can feel that the flesh is raised and sore.

At last the lock is ahead, No.17, Les Bellions. It has coloured lights to monitor the traffic in and off the Vilaine, and here I see once again with enormous pleasure this most beautiful river that made such an impression on me on a trip to Rieux a year ago. I remember standing on the bank with a lump in my throat as I watched the sun on the wide, wide water and the sailing boats drifting by.

After a last rest, I shoulder what seems by now an

impossibly heavy pack and set off, stiff-jointed, along the canal, which twists away from the Vilaine here to follow its own sad path up to Redon. The channel gets narrower and narrower, frequently blocked by spreading and prolific weeds. The contrast with the Vilaine is telling: through the trees I catch a glimpse of a white-sailed yacht on the river, a symbol of free-flowing movement and the current of life.

The railway carrying the main line from Redon to Nantes is soon running alongside to the right of the canal, and the situation, after hours and hours of orange towpath is strangely disorientating. To the left is a railing and a steep sheer drop into the canal far below, whilst to the right is the wall of the railway track itself with all the cabling visible above. So my path is on a sort of intermediary level, with a sense of no-man's land. There's something compelling that seems to pose the choice here: what's it to be, drowning or electrocution? This is the first time I've seen canal and railway so close together, highlighting their reversal of the legendary tortoise and hare story. This setting decisively breaks the connection of canal and countryside, in an emphatic statement of industrial purpose. But it's hard to imagine any boats bringing this section of the canal alive again.

At a small disused road bridge now going nowhere, the towpath ceases and a narrow tarmac road leads all the way up to St-Nicolas-de-Redon. The hard smack of foot on tarmac jolts my knee into familiar patterns of pain. It's a shame but probably not unfitting, to end this trip on several kilometres of road walking along a useless, dead canal.

Chapter 4   Canal Central

"The single biggest problem in communication is the illusion that it has taken place"

G.B.Shaw

Another month, another trip, and I pick up exactly where I left off. The kilometre from St-Nicolas into Redon is along the straight stretch of La Digue, where a very busy main road lined with large commercial outlets runs beside the towpath. It is pouring with rain as I trudge into this canal town, famous for its confluence of waterways and the Abbaye St-Sauveur founded by Conwoïon in 832, a foundation at the heart of the vigorous events of 9th century Brittany. The first sight of the striking Romanesque tower ahead makes up for the weather.

This strategic position on the Oust and Vilaine rivers was exploited at least as early as the period of Roman occupation. The later growth of its prestigious abbey, enriched by duties on water-borne traffic, contributed to the importance and renown of Redon, which also became a focus of pilgrimage. The relics of Saint Marcellin (given by Pope Leo IV to Conwoïon), were later enhanced by those of Conwoïon himself, who died at Plélan in 868. For the faithful travelling from England, Redon was also a stopping point on the Compostella trail - a legacy explicit in the Quai St-Jacques (where there was once a chapel to the saint), whence embarkation for the pilgrims. Above the small memorial to this role on the quay are remnants of the impressive 14th century town ramparts. In the second half of the 15th century, Redon was even the seat of government, as the Etats de Bretagne were regularly summoned to meet in a building which now houses La Bogue restaurant in the Rue des Etats.

Redon's position on the Vilaine, its tidal water providing access for sea-faring ships, made it in effect the port of Rennes, one of the capital cities of Brittany, and a major centre of trade. Before the silting up of the river channel, it was accessible to large three-masted vessels, which were unloaded here and their goods taken on by barge on the Vilaine. The inland situation protected the port from direct outside threat, but English blockades in 1760 brought trade on the Vilaine to a standstill, with resultant hardship for the inhabitants of Redon.

Despite this, trade generally proliferated in the 18th century, as the town was the market centre for the surrounding areas as well as a site of transit for the important salt trade. In 1785 a municipal plan to widen streets for improved circulation of traffic resulted in the loss of many old half-timbered houses and the creation of new roads such as the Rue des Etats and Rue Nominoë. An older street, the Rue de la Châtaigneraie, a name dating back to the 14th century, is a reminder of the ancient importance of the versatile chestnut in this area, a fruit still celebrated here every October in a special festival.

Athough Redon's later epithet 'Venise de l'Ouest' owes more to a vivid marketing imagination than visual reality, the interest of the town's history lies in this mélange of spiritual, political and economic roles. *Petite ville, grand renom* - another proud sobriquet - is a more simply evocative and accurate description. It is certainly a place where one is inevitably prompted to dwell on the many-faceted nature of communication.

The Vilaine is broad, grey and powerful here under stormy skies. The canal crosses it at right-angles: it is hard to imagine the manoeuvres and effort required to get over that seething river and back into the still waters of the artificial channel. By contrast the Port du Plaisance is calm and colourful today with the Welsh flag much in evidence for some reason.

Between this *bassin*, a 19th creation, and the Vilaine lies the old port area, a network of narrow streets lined with former warehouses and merchants' houses. Salt from Guerande was an important commodity: the early 17th century salt *greniers* stand opposite the Passage des Saulniers which leads directly to the waterside where the port was once situated. A walk along the Quai Duguay Trouin reveals handsome buildings with wrought-iron balconies originally belonging to *armateurs* who used the ground floors to store their wares. Wine, spices, salt, fabrics, fish, iron and building stone were all brought in, with wood, slate, grain and linen the prime exports. Thanks to this vibrant trade, even the *Compagnie des Indes orientales* found it worth their while to have an office, if not permanent premises, here at the end of the 18th century.

The opening of the Nantes-Brest canal through Redon fifty years later breathed new life into the port, but for only a short time. Industry and naval workshops had grown up on the banks of the Vilaine - in 1830 200 people were employed in the construction of ships, but this enterprise declined with the coming of the railway in 1862, and ship-building began to be concentrated in Lorient and St-Nazaire.

I'm stopping here in Redon overnight to reacquaint myself with the town, and decide to take a stroll southwards along the Vilaine, as ominously dark clouds continue to mass overhead. At the end of the quay near the Port aux Vins are two *hôtels* of the 17th century, including the handsome 'Tour de Richelieu', its name a reflection of the time when the Cardinal, minister of Louis XIII, was *abbé commendataire* in Redon.

At the point where the entrance to the current port divides from the Vilaine stands the Croix des Marins, today silhouetted dramatically against a deep grey sky lit from behind by streaks of sunlight. The path here is called the *Chemin sous la mare* - fortunately not so at this time, but the threat of the turbulent water churning a couple of metres from my feet is implicit. I find its power hypnotic and linger at the edge for a long while, thinking of the precarious nature of man's trust in water as a means of transport.

Returning up the Quai Jean Bart, I reach the Musée de la Batellerie behind two enormous lock-gates. The canal as a piece of social and economic history which repays study is clearly enshrined here, and the museum contains a wealth of information for canaloracs. There's a thorough video presentation of life on the canals (with an English version), a strong reminder that this long channel of water was a way of life for many people over many years. Numerous photographs, documents and artefacts demonstrate the workings of the system and there is even an inter-active model that enables the visitor to move a boat through a lock.

Inside the museum, administrator and curator Charly Bayou is manfully holding forth to a group of typical teenagers and their resigned teachers. Creeping around behind the motor engines from early boats, my ex-teacher's heart goes out to him and I long to call out the answers that are completely unforthcoming from his audience. A man who changed the history of France and Europe? Silence. Early 19th century? Nothing. A Corsican? That familiar mixture of despair and impatience sets in - little chap? No, not one of these youngsters can name Napoleon.

The results are more amusing when he gets on to numbers and calculating how long journeys on the canal would have taken. Everyone feels more confident with figures: pupils readily suggest lengths of the canal varying from 2000 odd kilometres to a few metres. In fact, Charly's very good at presenting the information clearly and pitching it at a level they should appreciate. It's not total apathy or ill-nature he's up against, just mental idleness, an inability to listen carefully for more than five seconds and a total disregard for anything older than yesterday.

When the youngsters are settled to chat to each other in front of the film about life on the canals, he has time to talk. He has described me to them as an English visitor and when I take him to task about this, he acknowledges the assumption with a grin and makes up for it by getting out a book of old ledgers to show me the amount of business Redon did with Swansea (my family's home town) and other south Wales settlements, particularly the pine pit-props for the mines and return cargoes of coal. His easy and engaging enthusiasm makes him a very fit guardian of the canal's memorabilia.

I leave him to sort out the school party for an hour. When I come back, the teenagers are all energetically leaping into their coach. Charly looks tired. I appreciate the time he gives me when he'd probably prefer the calming exercise of quietly watching fish weaving their sinuous patterns in the museum's aquarium.

A brief lull in the harsh weather encourages me to leave the Abbey, which I've visited several times before, for the next morning, but I've seen a reference in an old guidebook to a statute of Conwoïon at a fine look-out point on the Butte de Beaumont, and judge this worth the climb through residential streets. I imagine a leafy haven with stunning views over the town. The reality couldn't be more different. Hideous blocks of flats have been built in front of the statue, which actually stands in a few square metres of dusty shrubs beside a road. The symbolic portrayal of the abbey's founder is not surprisingly an idealised fantasy of the saintly and statesmanlike Conwoïon - his appearance reminds me a little of Cicero, although I'm sure the monk with his close connections to the powers-that-were had a more definite political line than that old trimmer. I plod downhill again.

The Hotel Le France is cheap, central, and right by the canal, which I can see from my window, and Patrick Franco is a helpful and pleasant host. Communications are preoccupying me at the moment. I'm waiting for an email message, and having established that there's telephone access but no WiFi at the hotel for my own computer, I go off in search of a cyber café. Not far from the tourist office is an internet access point packed with young people chatting online and playing noisy cyber games, swinging back and forth with the repressed energy of the physically inactive on the black faux-leather chairs. No message for me, at least not the one I need, but enough of routine business and casual acquaintance to while away the 15 minutes I've paid for. Returning in the evening to try again, I find the place even busier. The appearance is of concentrated communication, but is a screen a real substitute for human contact? I'd settle for it now, but there's still no message. I console myself with some strong cider and watch a football match on the TV in my hotel room.

In the morning there's clearly been a huge amount of rainfall and it's still lashing the windows of the hotel as a howling wind stirs up all manner of debris through the streets. Fearing that further exploration of the town is doomed, I take my time over breakfast, but amazingly within quarter of an hour the sky has cleared and the rain finally stops. I wander up Grande Rue with its ancient colombage houses (now sporting telecom signs and the like) and then dip under the railway by the Hotel de Ville, past the tourist office, intending to consult the internet yet again. The place is closed. It is supposed to open at 10 and it's 10.17. I wander around aimlessly and then return. 10.37. Still closed. Starting off on another little circuit I come across yet another similar business, only a few metres round the corner from the first. Not only that but it's cheaper, more welcoming and, most importantly of all, open. Still no message.

This form of communication is a tricky business: distance and silence render email a lethal emotional weapon. The fundamental concept of messages is a two-way process, essentially a dialogue of shared information, but how often does it descend into *magister dixit* mode, and how rarely is an accurate reflection of feeling conveyed. Studies show that we glean 93% of 'emotional meaning' from an interlocutor's tone of voice and facial expression - in other words only 7% from what is actually said to us. What hope does this hold out for email, that stark, cold medium, and cyber chat? Study of any internet chatroom will demonstrate how easily and wilfully we misunderstand each other, and this scope for self-destruction raises a problem in the context of language as a key tenet of identity. Groups consisting of people with shared interests and experiences all too easily generate vicious slanging matches over an odd misinterpreted word. But then, what hope for words at all when smileys are becoming a substitute for the infinite variety of language? Speed is the key now - we must transmit our feelings, our desires, our requests quickly and stripped of subtlety.

In not dissimilar fashion the brash train outran the canal when the railway arrived in Redon, and as speed gradually became the *sine qua non* of commerce and communication, all the slowly shifting nuances of gentle movement and human contact faded. Walking the canal restores a little sense of that lost quality of leisurely involvement with one's surroundings and connection with the landscape.

In the Tourist Office I have a positively pleasant encounter with a very helpful and alert young woman, who is interested in what I'm doing, and shows a rare awareness of the potential of her role. This is something I feel strongly about, having worked in tourist offices in England, and it always takes me by surprise here in Brittany when staff are often disinterested, monosyllabic and without a shred of curiosity. The impression that they are doing you a favour in doling out miniscule snippets of information - and sometimes misinformation - seems so common that one sometimes wonders if it's part of the training.

A friend who was staying with me some years ago went on a Saturday to the tourist office in Sizun, which is opposite the beautiful church and parish close, to enquire about church services. Yes, he was told, there's a service at 10.30 on Sundays. He set off the next morning but returned soon after to say there was no - decidedly unspiritual word - service. Out of curiosity we went back to the tourist office when it was next open. Yes, he was assured by the same person, there is a service at 10.30 on Sundays - but it's only every other week. A fact she clearly knew all along, but obviously regarded as privileged information. In some tourist offices here (others are excellent, of course) only thumb screws would extract full disclosure. I imagine a tourism mogul rallying his troops with the slogan LESS IS MORE.

Here in Redon on this dull, chilly day I have a properly useful exchange, a model of equal communication. The assistant provides me with the information I want, managing at the same time to give me the impression that Redon is an excellent place, well worth publicising, and she then asks about my work and the possibility of the office stocking the concise canal guide when it's ready, because *it would benefit*

51

their visitors - a rare flower in the desert, this young woman. I come away thinking again about communication and wonder if it isn't an art or perhaps an innate skill, because all the training in the world is not going to artificially create a fundamental desire to provide service or the instinct to engage and share beyond the basic requirements of politeness. It can't be done by rote.

I have some very good coffee in a salon de thé in Grande-Rue and watch the many young people drifting about the streets, full of life and mirth, their body language voluble. By middle-age we've lost this spontaneous form of expression, guarding ourselves more carefully, weighing and checking our channels of communication, perhaps because we know the potential consequences, but youth is all open, swinging arms, relaxed clothing, easy physical contact between peers. I enjoy watching them and listening to their badinage as I stroll behind a lively group up to the Abbey. Many more are hanging around outside the entrance, presumably waiting for their classes in the adjoining lycée to begin. After the museum experience, I wonder if any of them could tell me the story of this ancient edifice if I asked, or if they've ever been inside.

When I go in, I have the place entirely to myself on this chilly morning. The contrast between the dark Romanesque nave and a bright - over-bright? - gothic altar is overwhelming, especially as nature is providing the sort of glaring lighting suited to an artificial film-set, with sudden strident rays of sun shooting through the plain glass windows. Shifting swathes of dust particles through which this glittering spectacle is visible add a further dramatic touch. It really is an abbey of two separate halves and its grandiose size does not help to connect them: St-Philibert-le-Grand, a roughly contemporary structure in Loire-Atlantique is smaller, which lends a unity lacking here.

The foundation of the abbey at Redon came at an exciting time in Breton history. Repeated and unsuppressible outbreaks of resistance to the imposition of Frankish rule in the early 9th century had led the emperor of the Franks,

Louis le Pieux, to try another method of containment. The appointment of Nominoë, a Breton, as *missus imperatoris* in the region led to a period of truce which fostered the development of Breton confidence and perhaps of a discrete identity in the face of the potentially swamping political and cultural force of the Franks, emanating from a Latinised east.

Conwoïon and his six companions were given land for their religious foundation by the *machtiern* (local chief) Ratuili, but retrospective permission at a higher level had to be obtained and the fledging abbey faced opposition from the religious establishment at Vannes. When the emperor appeared to drag his feet and twice rebuffed Conwoïon as he sought a personal audience, it was Nominoë who stepped in decisively and ratified the abbey's tenure in 834. A few months later the emperor followed his appointee's lead - he could hardly have done otherwise, as Nominoë must have been shrewd enough to realise. On the other hand, Benedictine rule was adopted very early in the abbey's development, in line with the will of Louis, who had already imposed this on the abbey of Landevennec in 818.

The abbey suffered similar fortunes to others in the region in the subsequent centuries: monks fleeing Viking raiders, damage during the wars of succession for the dukedom of Brittany and suppression at the time of the revolution. In fact the church itself was almost destroyed by fire in 1780 and then rebuilt on a smaller scale - hence the odd position of the single 14th century bell-tower.

I wander into the adjoining cloister, another relic of Richelieu's time in office, and find it a little disappointing, the atmosphere lost by busy foot traffic to and from the lycée. The upper part of the construction is in blocks of tuffeau brought by water from the Loire area to the port of Redon. From this courtyard, however, there is the best view of the Romanesque tower, one of the finest examples of the style in Brittany, built at the bidding of Alain Fergent, the last Breton-speaking duke of Brittany, who ruled at the end of the 11th century. After five years crusading, he passed the dukedom to his son and retired to the abbey here for a contemplative life. The indivisibility of politics and religion at that time makes this an unsurprising fact: compare the feat of imagination required to picture Nicolas Sarkozy passing his remaining years in a monastery.

The most valuable historical legacy of the abbey at Redon is its *cartulaire*, a manuscript dating from the 9th to the 11th century, produced in Carolingian script by monks in the abbey's scriptorium. This remarkable document was saved from destruction after the Revolution: the abbey papers were being shipped to Rennes for burning when the barge carrying them ran aground and the cartulaire was mysteriously rescued by an unknown hand. It came into the possession of the abbey of St-Melaine in Rennes and is still retained in the diocesan archives there today.

The cartulaire contains a wealth of information primarily about the abbey's land holdings - extending all over Brittany and beyond to the east - and dealings with tenants. After the anarchic years of Viking invasions - when the monks were forced to abandon the abbey at Redon temporarily - the recorded statements of property and possessions became of legal significance. Disputes of ownership were not uncommon: Belle-Isle, for example, was claimed not only by the abbey of Redon but also that of Quimperlé, which led to clear falsifications of dates in records at both ends of the argument. From the cartulaire come intricate historical details of land measures, social structures and economic preoccupations. It is also an onomastic treasure trove of early Breton, with over 800 place names and more than 2000 personal names.

Nominoë's importance to the early establishment of the abbey is recorded. He never took or had bestowed the title *roi*, although this is routinely claimed in casual history, but the cartulaire - and in what better source would one expect to find such a title if it existed? - refers to him only as *duc* and *prince*. (His son Erispoë did gain recognition from Charles le Chauve and took the title of King, but it was a short-lived phenomon in Brittany. Alain le Grand was the last to hold this title a little more than fifty years later.)

Nominoë doesn't need elevation to royal status to acknowledge his role in Breton history: the actions we know of are indicative of a natural desire for expanding and securing his spheres of power and influence and rejecting the assumptive authority of the Franks. What he thought and felt is unknown, but today he is used as a means of conveying messages about a supposed (and surely anachronistic) concept of Breton identity and has become a posthumous soldier in the modern cause of nationalism.

After Louis' death in 840, Nominoë was soon at odds with his successor Charles le Chauve. Energetic raids on the eastern borders made clear the Breton determination to wrest control of the marches of Brittany from the Franks. Charles' large-scale military effort to put a stop to this came to grief at Ballon (Bains-sur-Oust) just to the north of Redon, where the light-armed Bretons on their dexterous horses hopped and skipped to victory. This 'glorious' achievement has been extolled by some historians and Breton nationalists as a decisive moment in the establishment of that alluring chimaera, the Breton identity. What it certainly did was to free the Bretons from direct rule by the Franks/French for nearly seven hundred years. Some indication of Nominoë's thinking is given by his removal of bishops appointed by the Franks - on charges of simony - and replacing them with Bretons in 849, in addition to creating a new archbishopric at Dol-de-Bretagne, muscle-flexing exercises of both religious and political significance.

No known likeness of the enigmatic Nominoë exists. His historical personage has been usurped by some Breton nationalists, the life and colour of his individualism drained to the glum symbol that stands as a stylised statue in nearby Bains-sur-Oust today. With politicisation of identity comes the triumph of rhetoric over instinct, the assertion of declaration over sincerity of sentiment.

My predominant image of Redon will always remain one of water, the seething force of the Vilaine and the quiet redundancy of the canal, but walking out of the town to an obligato of light rain, reminders of this essentially urban environment are unavoidable in a rash of grim litter all along the banks of the towpath. The noise of traffic and machinery is strident, keeping up the impression of a certain frenetic busyness, of going somewhere, that befits a centre of communications. Junctions proliferate with bridges and roundabouts everywhere and an all-pervading sense of movement and activity. Whether arrival is productive or desirable is another matter.

The tarmac towpath feels mushy, its top layer soft underfoot. The water level is low here, exposing large blocks of rubble. Below the opposite bank are patches of a lurid green substance that has been emptied into the canal: it looks disgusting. It is in fact a depressingly grim section leaving Redon. Suddenly the towpath seems to peter out, forcing a detour along a very busy main road with lorries hurtling in both directions. I can see a path continuing on the other side of canal and wonder about going back to the last bridge and giving it a try. That side of the water is open countryside, with glimpses of a church spire and low wooded hills, an idyll compared to the commercial and industrial mayhem over here. Yet another deluge of rain forces me to retrace my steps to the bridge just for shelter, and I sit on a concrete step studying maps until the worst is over.

I decide to brave the road when the torrent abates a little, but it is not a happy choice. Traffic flies by about a foot away sending up sheets of water and grit. I climb over the metal barrier and try to make my way along the steep, slippery bank, clinging painfully onto the rimmed metal with one hand, struggling to keep the weight of my pack steady and avoid dropping into the water below. Others have clearly carved out this dangerous route and presumably survived, but I'm scared, although the ordeal lasts only a couple of hundred metres before the towpath separates again, just as the rain stops and all is suddenly well again. Now I can relax, knowing what is in store. I'm on my way to le Pont d'Oust near Peillac, but first I will pass through some of the most beautiful scenery the canal has to offer.

Chapter 5   Crossing the Line

*"I know the joy of fishes in the river through my own joy
as I walk along the same river"*
                                                Zhuangzi

At La Potinais, the canal meets the river Oust as it turns northward to dissect the falaises, sheer rock faces, around the Ile aux Pies. Here the towpath crosses to the south side just before the barrage spanning a wide expanse of water. Fittingly, the long-forgotten sun comes out over the strong flowing, broad river. I feel my body releasing its tension as all is verdant and bright, despite a black sky up ahead. A cow bathes lugubriously by the opposite bank as I follow a bulging bend made lovely by the muted greens of deciduous trees just on the turn: some remain bright, others are shedding yellow and brown spotted leaves onto the towpath. The promise of autumn is in sight and smell, with conkers, beech-mast and rosehips all in evidence.

This is the most tranquil and yet atmospheric walk on the canal so far. The river gets wider and wider, splitting around the Ile aux Pies, and the scenery more dramatic with a vertiginous, densely wooded hill to the right, and, unusually, a few huge fir trees dotted along the towpath. I sit on a rock overlooking the island to have my lunch, lulled into peace and a sense of harmony by the absorbing beauty of the scene.

Setting off again, the first of the falaises is soon in view, wonderful stark granite cliffs with a few skeletal outlines of fir trees. The transverse valley adopted by the river Oust here represents a geological fault zone in the granite mass of Lanvaux, which is visible further south in the form of wild and rough *landes*. Walking through this gorge is made impressive not so much by the height of the rocks but the breadth of the river. The grey and moody water matches the sky, which provides just the right quality of sombre light to add to the sense of natural wonder. It is like passing through a gateway into Brittany, the granite a fitting symbol for the country. I have a sudden sense of something beginning: the path westwards lies ahead - from Oust to West. A towering cliff-face appears, stark and foreboding. This area, 15kms of which is designated a Grand Site naturel, is a rock-climbers paradise with walls of schist and granite up to 50m high.

The spell of such striking scenery is broken at the approach to Lock 19, Le Painfaut, notable for its well-tended garden. Here the canal swings left to part from the meandering Oust for a few kilometres and a long, arrow-straight stretch lies ahead lined by poplars and beeches. There is nothing monotonous about the loveliness of trees: a sprightly breeze dances around their slim, elegant trunks and sings through the leaves. This is truly walking with one's ears - the birds, the water and the wind all contributing their lines to the music. A navy-blue painted boat called Rivendell is moored at the bank. After the next deserted lock, its gates standing open, the Oust rejoins the canal and welcome wiggles of natural river break up the narrow view. Walking beside the broad river and the luxuriant trees here is to participate in a rural idyll, finally broken by the sight of a line of flags - Welsh dragon to the forefront - at the approach to Pont d'Oust.

I make an early start from Peillac, in brooding and melancholy mood despite the astonishing beauty of the scene. Mist drifts across the water as if the river is exhaling under shafts of gentle sunlight, and the coldly autumnal air around my legs contrasts with a blue sky and bright clouds. The path is narrow and muddy through grass for a short way before widening into the customary track. The countryside unfolds, open and generous in its *richesse*. The sight of bright red rosehips makes sentimental tears well up as if I'd walked into the scene of a poem by one of the early Romantics. It is true that my thoughts are in my eyes today. Those long thoughts are back, twisting the screw of identity and intention: subconsciously I am feeling unsettling shifts of direction in my life. There is a time in every journey when arrival must be acknowledged and the place of that arrival explored. One cannot always be passing through, in perpetual transit. I think I believe that travel radiating from a solid base-camp gives the best combination of security and possibility - it's finding the place to pitch the tent that's elusive. I fear the claustrophobia of grinding to a premature halt. But if unhappiness is usually the result of feeling stuck and powerless, walking has its benefits. Forward movement maintains a sense of progress and possibility.

The old adage *solvitur ambulando* - essentially the validation of theory by practical experience, but just as useful a life-tool in solving problems by walking - comes to mind and psychologically I put my foot down whilst trying not to forge ahead physically without sense of my surroundings, something I'm prone to when in the throes of the long thought. So I bring back my focus to a dovecote in a field across the water, a structure smaller and slimmer than is customary. I look out for the château it must belong to, which appears, an unremarkable structure in a superb setting, a little later on as a hawk mews over the flat farmland to my left.

At the next lock, Le Gueslin, two fishermen sit at a camping table, backs to their lines, sharing bread, sausage and what looks like a large bottle of whisky. I've seen an old photo of this lock-house in which the lock-keeper in working smock and flat hat stands outside, holding his little daughter by the hand, whilst his tightly smiling wife and four other children pose stoically for the camera. It's a reminder of the former real life of this canal, its functional purpose, of which there is little sense today, and a lost time when contact with the outside world must have been a welcome change. Now lock-houses are often in private hands and some owners ostentatiously avoid contact with passers-by who interrupt their isolated existence. Being separate has become more sought-after and desirable in an age where there is far too much easy contact with the world through television and computers, too many people and casual contacts in our lives with the massive increase in movement brought by cars.

Why is there never a seat when one is tired? It's a sort of law of canal walking - seats manifest in inverse proportion to one's energy levels. As I am passing the settlement of St-Martin on the opposite side of the river, I shall call this St-Martin's Law. There have been seats along this stretch - this is not Loire Atlantique after all - but nothing at the moment when I need rest. Always, not wanting to sit on the wet ground, I walk on the extra two or three kilometres that takes away the benefit of the short rest when it eventually comes. Today, despite my left knee getting stiffer and stiffer, my spirits finally lift with the quiet peace, and through the beech boughs a sky the colour of cornflowers. A bench made of two logs finally appears by a little access road in open countryside: I sit and look at hamlets, farmland, grazing cows and then the water, enjoying a tranquil awareness of all the varied creatures who call the canal home.

By contrast a stretch of the noise, smell and waste of commercial activity begins soon after. An enormous agro-industrial plant, whitewashed and shaped like an ocean-liner complete with funnel looms just off the tow-path. From the outside it looks smart, functional and relentlessly modern, a most unsuitable bed-fellow for the canal. I'd rather not know what goes on inside.

Before reaching St-Congard, where the same sort of enterprises line the opposite bank on approach, I pass a significant spot in canal history: the old quay at Port d'Oust was where the last working boat, The Mistral, unloaded its final cargo of sand in December 1977. Just beyond, at St-Congard itself, the din of timber yards is so invasive that I decide not to take my scheduled rest here. What a burden to hang over the lives of the inhabitants! I'm also dismayed by the first in a series of semi-jokey notice-boards about life on the canal in its heyday, supposedly narrated by a young man who likes fishing. This is not about reality but well-chosen facts and figures to present an up-beat image of the canal and its past. Why is it assumed that we all have to be amused before our interest is engaged? I don't expect life on or by the canals was generally a barrel of laughs in the 19th century.

This is not a pleasant bit of walking. A little further ahead bright red water is streaming into the canal from a quarry site just to the west. Everywhere the earth is this sienna colour. This must surely be laying down a deep bed of sediment under the water. The quarry is extensive, with large bites gouged out of the escarpment as if a giant had been snacking. It's an ugly defacement of nature to repay her bounty. Further on the din from a food production plant is overwhelming: again water carrying who knows what waste products appears to pour directly into the canal.

I want to stop for a good rest before the last long stretch to Malestroit and so try out various perches on fallen trees and odd stones before moving restlessly on in the hope of something better. Suddenly I decide abruptly to stop where I am regardless and collapse onto the knobbly base of a tree. Almost instantly I'm rewarded for the decision by the sight of two kingfishers, startlingly blue and a flash of red as they curve in front of me and into the bank below. Some animal - presumably a *ragondin*, that rapacious South-American immigrant - has strewn a trail of corncobs from the field behind across the towpath and down to the water. Later I see a pair, whiskered snouts and rumps protruding above the water, in a swampy area just off the canal. Originally introduced at the end of the 19th century for their fur, the *ragondin* was later regarded as useful for keeping down vegetation that might clog up lakes. The good life led to an inevitable population explosion, however, and the coypu is now an unattractive destructive nuisance, destabilising river-banks and unpoisonable for fear of harming more welcome mammals like the appealing otter. It's a hard luck story of a kind.

After a lone day's walking seeing only two cyclists, it's stimulating to reach a town, especially one as inviting as Malestroit, and to see people going about their normal everyday business. Children are having canoe lessons from the steps of a sports ground opposite the towpath: the instructor gives a nonchalant 'o la' as one young lad overturns and falls out into the water. He is left to get his craft - much bigger than himself - upright again and swim to shore pushing it ahead. A group of nurses wheeling elderly patients beside the water are easily over-taken by young mothers with bent backs briskly pushing their baby-buggies ahead in a sort of race for life.

I am breaking my journey here and turn off the canal at once into streets of half-timbered medieval houses with their decorative wood carvings, like the hare playing *biniou* or Breton bagpipes. What soon puts me off lingering in the centre is the gratuitous noise echoing stridently around the streets. More and more little towns seem to have these loud-speaker systems broadcasting crappy music to all and sundry whether they want it or not. Here it's not even music, but an interview of some sort blaring out over the fine architecture - what a telling clash between solid history and vapid modernity. It's as if quiet is potentially harmful, a vacuum that must be filled. The lack of sound creates a kind of fear, as if we are afraid to hear only the echo of our own emptiness. Canal walking provides a perfect type of quiet - silence edged by bird song and gentle water movement, the music of nature. But even the canal has seen its own degrees of silence change with time, from the rhythmic clop of hooves to the motorised boats that began to replace horses well before WWII. Faster movement and more noise - the start of the modern world. Ironically, the canal lost its purpose and thereby regained its peace.

Across the Oust, past the old mills, the ruins of La Madeleine stand on a slight rise. This chapel dates back to the 12th century, but is best known as the venue for the signing of the Treaty of Malestroit. In January 1343, watched over by papal legates, representatives of the French king, Philippe de Valois, and Edward III of England put signatures to a document which brought a temporary lull in the Breton War of Succession and the release from prison of the English-backed claimant Jean de Montfort. The energetic actions of his wife, Jeanne de Flandre had helped to keep his cause alive in spite of his captivity. In fact it was his son, another Jean, who was finally to grasp the dukedom unequivocally after the Battle of Auray in which Charles de Blois, champion of the Breton side, was killed.

A less well-known event in the chapel's history is recorded in a later painting by Alexandre Bloch, a still death one might call it, which shows the lofty interior of the chapel calm in gentle light until one's eyes are drawn to the almost unobtrusive bodies on the floor. They are Chouans, members of the Catholic anti-revolutionary, pro-royalist rebels so strongly represented in Morbihan after the Revolution put an end to their world, five of them killed here in Malestroit by French government forces despite a desperate struggle in 1795. I suppose it was a fitting place for defenders of the faith to end their lives.

Leaving Malestroit on a grey, cold morning the water looks tired and dusty but the trees are exceptionally beautiful - beech, poplar and oak. I feel physically fit today and a lot more mentally relaxed. Shiny conkers and beech-mast littering the path are reminders of autumn pushing in with clearer air and a range of hues unmatched in any other season.

A wonderful tableau: I am watching a heron motionless on the bank as a cyclist comes up very fast indeed behind. Brian the dog is with me, well ahead, but he does not panic and stands quietly while the man rushes by. The heron is disturbed and glides away. An ensemble of movement results, the moment after the still life encapsulated: Brian stock still, the bike whizzing and the heron gliding between them. A fine juxtaposition of the natural and unnatural. Biking seems to me movement as a form of exercise, something utilitarian - at the speed he was travelling it would be impossible to take in any detail of the surroundings or environment.

Coming up to Lock 28 Ville-aux-Fruglins, the rain starts in earnest although the sky is quite light. Fishermen on the lock look the epitome of contented stillness. I on the other hand like travelling and the sense - perhaps false sense - of progress that it generates. I always want to be getting somewhere and am not good at remaining motionless in any sense. Walking reflects this reluctance to be still, a desire for constant sense of purpose and achievement, but this very movement can be an isolating process. It's no good asking me for an aimless stroll. Stagnation is a deeply rooted fear, which is perhaps why I have no affinity with fishermen. But drive has its drawbacks, the greatest for me being a separation from the recuperative power of passivity. The Hanged Man of tarot: sometimes it is necessary to let go and wait - here's the hard bit - without specific anticipation. Let the world swim by and wait for natural flow to pick you up again: meanwhile, enjoy the rest and let the mind out of its strait-jacket to roll around freely. I'm reluctant to believe fishermen further along the path of human evolution than the rest of us: maybe they are all inwardly seething with thwarted ambition or plotting to murder their wives under that peaceful veneer.

Before the use of horses, many bargemen, wearing a special harness, pulled their own vessels along the canal. I have no distance figures for this phenomenon but I cannot imagine progress was swift. Upgrading to animal power meant a horse-drawn boat could cover up to 25kms a day and when motorised boats largely replaced this method from the 1930s, speed of travel on the canal increased a further three or fourfold. A noticeboard here explains the procedure for horse-drawn boats passing: whichever was moving with the current had priority and the other boat simply had to un-harness its horse and tie up at the bank. This manoeuvre must have been repeated again and again on a day's journey at the height of traffic on the canal.

At La Roche André, with its imposing chapel high above the water, the towpath crosses the fine thirteen arch 18th century road bridge, part of the Duc d'Aiguillon's plans for improving the road network in Brittany, and regains the northern bank of the river. Passing a sawmill, I walk through a miasma of that distinctive smell of sawn wood and wood shavings and the air is full of tiny chips of wood that sting the eyes.

To my right is the Château du Crévy (now a costume museum I discover later) with its extensive walled enclosure and elaborate modern jetty. This is an incredibly lovely section of walking. Huge pine trees line the towpath and I can see the lock of Montertelot ahead, an oasis of tranquil beauty. A little chapel with tiny fontaine and ancient houses are right by the canal where the water opens out into a huge channel with many pleasure boats moored. I stop here for a picnic lunch and will long remember the sense of refreshment and well-being that spot was generous enough to provide. An old man wobbles past several times on a bike which clearly has the upper hand, although I suspect they've been together for many years. He smiles warmly each time and finally wishes me 'bon appetit' before lurching off between houses.

Setting off again as the rain renews, I discover the loss of my favourite hat, last seen several kilometres back, too far to retrace my steps in search of it. I am even more than usually ashamed of the strident blue poncho, as another pair of kingfishers treat me to a glimpse of nature's vibrant palette. This is excellent walking still, despite the weather, or even enhanced by it, because there's no doubt in my mind after so many hours of canal walking that rain suits it very well and brings out the smells, sounds and shades of colour admirably. The towpath is oddly wide like a road for a time on this lonely stretch with only the birds in range of my senses and the unusual sight of a weeping willow on the far bank.

By the time I pass Lock 30, Blond, the rain has stopped and it is really quite hot. We seem to have moved from autumn to summer over 20 kilometres. The trees here are still richly green along the elegant bends of the Oust, lined by water-meadows and bucolically grazing cattle. Just after the next lock is some evidence of the extensive mill activity that used to characterise the Oust before the canal adversely affected the flow of water. The Moulin de Guillac still appears to be in some sort of action, with lorries loading and a modern roll door and chute. The Moulin de Carmenais at the next lock too still produces flour from blé noir/sarrazin (buckwheat) and seigle - those traditional staples of the Breton diet - supplying crêperies and pizzerias far and wide with their produce.

In the middle of nowhere, a tiny fontaine with statue of a saint, sits in a little garden with an inviting seat. Some loving hand has created a spot for human harmony with nature. A red squirrel runs across the clearing as we approach and Brian is beside himself with excitement, huffing and puffing in all directions long after the superior creature is well beyond his reach.

Some sections of the canal seem to align themselves more with one sense than another. Today it is sound again: the susurration of the wind in the poplars has a sharper tone than usual, perhaps as the leaves begin to dry out seasonally. The canal is playing its own particular symphony here: birds, trees, water, machinery and cars all contributing to the score. The harmony changes to a minor key as a storm brews and the river gets lively. Twigs crack and fall in the woods.

Between Malestroit and Josselin, I have somewhere crossed the linguistic line dividing, in an earlier age, the Breton-speaking Basse-Bretagne from eastern Brittany with its more direct Latin/French influences. The area was once larger in the 9th century under the leadership of Nominoë when the Vilaine and the Couesnon formed a north/south boundary nearer Rennes. The legacy is clear in toponyms. From a multitude of small settlements called La Ville something, the ubiquitous Breton prefixes *ker* (hamlet or village) *plou/pleu* (parish) and *pen* (end/head) begin to appear: Kerfourn, Kergras, Penhouet, Pleugriffet. There is also a fair scattering of place-names ending in -ac, such as Guillac, deriving ultimately from the Gallic suffix -acon through the Gallo-Roman suffix (-acum). Further west, under the influence of British immigrants in the early centuries that laid the foundations of Breton, this has become -oc, or -euc, later on - ec. There are layers to excavate in language as there are in landscape. Indeed language belongs to the land, and in place-names lies the identity of the landscape. For me this descriptive hymn of topography is the true hold of Breton, and a reminder that identity was based on local landscape in the days when people travelled little outside their own communities. For walkers these names are precious signposts to the past.

Before the next road bridge is a welcome picnic table and of all things a canal-side boules court. I lie down gratefully and rest, remembering an earlier visit to a nearby monument. A little further on at St-Gobrien, the D123 crosses the canal and just to the north will go under the motorway very close to the Column of the Thirty in its wooded enclosure. This landmark commemorates a famous battle between knights in the 14th century War of Succession, a dispute over the dukedom of Brittany which had drawn the English onto Breton territory in defence of Jean de Montfort's claim. The French throne supported Charles de Blois who battled hard to keep the prize for his Penthièvre relations, cream of the Breton nobility.

Jean or Jehan de Beaumanoir was holding Josselin castle for the Bretons, whilst the English knight Thomas Bemborough was firmly ensconced in Ploërmel. An agreed combat between thirty knights on each side was arranged. This type of formalised fight was a common method of avoiding elaborate and uncontained battles. A typically bloody struggle followed in which all were either wounded or killed, but de Beaumanoir carried the day and led eighteen English prisoners back to Josselin. The encounter is enthusiastically chronicled by its contemporary Froissart, who later met one of the combatants, Yves Charruel:

Then out and spake Yves Charruel, with choler raging hot -
Betwixt the sea and where they stood a bolder knight was not:
"Perish the dastard vile I say, who tamely would go back,
And when his foes before him stand, would not those foes attack!"
(translation by William Harrison Ainsworth)

The story of the Battle of the Thirty is also relayed in various books and tourist information with a certain amount of gleeful relish, a raconteur's dream. This set-piece of

67

medieval warfare has become every bit as much a set-piece of Breton folklore. The reality is gruesome, the epitome of that stark brutality of the 14th century which saw living and dying by the sword as the most acceptable day-job. When de Beaumanoir's knights took dawn communion at the church of Notre-Dame-des-Ronciers before setting out for the chosen site of battle, they must have known that each and every one would sustain some wound, some disfigurement, some loss of limb if not life before the day was out. Charruel still bore the scars thirty years later. Hot and confined in their metal suits, with limited vision and heavy weaponry to wield against vicious opponents, were they frightened or excited? Resigned or trusting in their god? Probably a mixture of all those things. It was an age of excessive sensitivity, where men wept, fainted and saw visions with alarming regularity, coupled with the most grotesque and barbaric of violent acts.

Past the horse racing course, my first sight of Josselin is the spire of that very church where the knights prayed before their battle in 1351.

Chapter 6   Rohan Country

*"I like long walks, especially when they are taken by
people who annoy me."*
Fred Allen

On reaching Josselin, a town named after one of the
earliest counts of Porhoët, the canal flows past its huge
and impressive château, with only a narrow road separating
the walls from the water. Opposite is the Hôtel du Château,
now spruced up since I stayed there some years ago on my
first visit to this characterful medieval town.

Here one is entering the heartlands of Rohan territory, a
family which has played an exceptional role in the history of
Brittany. In the medieval period they controlled a fifth of the
land in the duchy with 63 parishes in Léon (north Finistère),
33 in Cornouaille (south Finistère) and 75 in central Brittany,
and regarded themselves as second to none, especially not
the usurping Montfort dukes of Brittany. Instrumental in
bringing the dukedom and Breton independence to an end in
1488 by siding with the king of France, Charles VIII, in the
Battle of St-Aubin-du-Cormier, they judged their interests to
be better served by alignment with the French cause than
offering allegiance to one of their peers.

Anne de Bretagne's marriage to the king of France soon
after was a bitter blow to Rohan hopes for supremacy in the
duchy, which they intended to secure through a marriage
alliance of their own. The French, however, no longer needed
to court Breton nobles with the same assiduousness and Jean
de Rohan found himself deposed as Lieutenant General in
favour of the prince of Orange. He soon joined with other
malcontented Breton nobles and looked to Henry VII of
England for aid, agreeing to open Morlaix and Brest to the
English in exchange. An English force was duly despatched
and then recalled as skilful French diplomacy resulted in a
treaty between France and England. Charles decided it
expedient to extend magnanimity to Jean de Rohan, offering
him a sizeable pension of 10,000 livres.

The 50 kilometre trek on the canal north-west from Josselin which I'm embarking on now also takes in the town of Rohan, their earliest stronghold in the 12th century and the lively centre of Pontivy, seat of Rohan power for hundreds of years. These three towns all bear the legacy of this puissant and distinctive family: the current Duc de Rohan and his family still occupy the château at Josselin.

The name Rohan derives from the Breton diminutive *roc'han*. From this 'little rock' the fame and fortune of the Rohan family has spread throughout Europe, where they have entered the highest echelons through marriage and enterprise. A document kept by the monks at Noirmoutier furnishes historical evidence for the founder member of the dynasty: 'I, Alain, viscount, have given to Saint-Martin and the monks from the monastery situated near to the Château of Josselin, all the bourg before the gate of my new castle called Rohan to build a church, cemetery and mill ...'

His son, Alain II was the first formally to carry the familial name 'de Rohan', and a new fortification at Pontivy, on the site of the current Château de Rohan, augmented the family holdings in the 12th century. A union in the next generation between Alain III de Rohan and Constance, sister of Duke of Brittany, Conan IV, saw the start of an extraordinary network of Rohan alliances, which was later to include the royal houses of Scotland, Navarre and Savoy as well as that of France.

During the War of Succession for the duchy of Brittany two hundred years later, when the Rohans took the side of Charles de Blois against the Montforts and their English supporters, both Rohan and Pontivy were taken and burned down by the Count of Northampton in 1342. When they regained their territories, Pontivy became the chief seat of the Rohans and the castle at Rohan was not rebuilt.

A byword for pride, the earliest motto of this family, found on a balustrade at the château of Josselin, was 'a plus' (to the highest) but more famous is the later 'Roi ne puis, Duc ne daigne, Rohan suis' - Can't be king, won't be prince, I'm a Rohan.' Although this powerful statement of identity did not originate with the Rohan family, its adoption was in keeping with their claim of descent from ancient Breton kings and subsequent ties by marriage with the highest nobility and royalty of Europe.

From the bridge by the château of Josselin, the picturesque Rue du Val d'Oust leads up into the town, or it is possible to turn back from it under an arch through the old ramparts to emerge by the château entrance. The stables rather incongruously now house a doll museum, displaying the large family collection from the last 150 years, a lowlier peg for Rohan achievement.

I stop off in the English Bookshop just here. This excellent shop is run by Jennifer and Martin Greene who have built a thriving business that serves both English and French customers and plays an important role in the community. I admire their energy and vision which have seen the business expand considerably at a time of life when many would prefer to be easing up a little. Jennifer shows me the latest renovation projects above the shop and kindly tells me that recently on the plane from England she sat next to someone who was reading one of my novels. The shop is certainly a well-stocked and welcoming place for book-lovers.

Once noted for its religious foundations, Josselin retains a fine church, the Basilica de Notre-Dame-du-Roncier, Our Lady of the Brambles. An account of 1666 tells the much earlier legend of a labourer who discovered a statue of Our Lady among the brambles he was clearing where the church now stands. He took it home but the statue returned to its former location. On hearing of this miracle, the Bishop of St-Malo authorized a new centre of worship. The labourer's daughter, blind from birth, recovered her sight after touching the statue, which led to flocks of pilgrims arriving to be healed. This story is told in the stained glass windows of the current church, which was rebuilt after the destruction of the town by Henry II Plantagenet in 1168 and 1171.

In the church is the tomb of Olivier de Clisson, Comte de Porhoët from 1370 until his death in 1407, former Constable of France and illustrious figure in the history of Josselin. He undertook some serious fortification of the castle, adding 9 towers and a huge keep. He was on bad terms with the Duke of Brittany, Jean IV, and not only because of his close connection with the French king: rumour had it that de Clisson was also involved with the duke's second wife, Jeanne Holland, *la belle Anglaise*, daughter of the Countess of Kent. De Clisson's tomb, in the chapel he himself had added to the church, was mutilated in the French Revolution and then later restored to its current state.

The château of Josselin had become more of a Rohan palace than a defensive stronghold by the 17th century as the family provided a bastion for Protestantism in staunchly Catholic Brittany during the Wars of Religion. In 1629 the keep and four towers were demolished on Cardinal Richelieu's orders after these savage conflicts - in which the Protestant Rohans were involved to the extent that the war was often called *les guerres de Monsieur de Rohan*. There is a story that Henri, then Duc de Rohan, ignored the order and Richelieu himself arrived at the château one day, greeting him with the words *'je viens, M le Duc, de jeter une boule dans votre jeu de quilles.'*

It's impossible to visit Josselin without being reminded of one of its most curious stories - that of *Les Aboyeuses*, or barking women. The original legend recounted how local washerwomen abused a female beggar who asked for alms, mocking her poor appearance and finally setting a dog on her. At this, she suddenly transformed into a 'dame de lumière' or Lady of Light, and for punishment cursed them and their daughters to bark like dogs. This vengeful story is not one the church has ever been particularly comfortable with, as it ill-befits the Virgin Mary's traditional image.

Historical developments include an event of 1728, when three children of Josselin fell to the ground 'barking like dogs'. Their father took them to the statue of Our Lady of the Brambles and they were at once healed. Science apparently provides its own explanation of a specific strain of epilepsy, but there are plenty of 19th century tales of women, overcome with frenzy and howling - often at the processions of Pentecost - who then have to touch the Virgin's robe or the reliquary containing remains of her first statue in order to be restored to calm. Old black and white postcards portray mad-eyed, white-capped females who regularly succumbed to this bizarre malady.

I am walking this part of the route during a period of *chômage* when the artificial parts of the canal are drained for maintenance work. In the old days this used to take place during summer months, which gave an enforced holiday to canal folk, but now when the only sporadic traffic is the pleasure boat trade, the tourist season has to be avoided and autumn is preferred. Leaving Josselin, the water is at its lowest level, revealing the schist bed and pipework running along the channel. Work is in progress on the next lock gate, which is being stripped and repaired: pieces of worn and saturated timber are strewn on the ground.

Where the Oust and canal split, an egret rises and flies off over the trees. Minutes later I come as close as I have ever done (and this is saying something considering hundreds of close encounters experienced on the Somerset Levels) to a grey heron who is absolutely still on the bank beside me. He seems unbothered by my silent presence, but as soon as there are footsteps on the path behind and the murmur of voices, he rises nonchalantly, flaps across the water and settles on the opposite bank, studiously looking away from the noisy humans who have interrupted his concentration. The elderly couple out for a stroll exclaim at their sighting and then struggle, pantomime-style with a recalcitrant umbrella as drops of rain begin to fall.

The dark red towpath rolls on ahead, past a lock right under the expressway with all its clamour and vibration, and then out into farmland. There are plenty of seats along this route, as if it's well-used. People probably come out just to admire the row of beautiful mature beech trees lining the way. Locks are closer together too as the land rises: before the next there are swirls of green sludge in the water, tracing a pattern like that made by a spirograph. A flock of geese fenced in with their own stretch of water presumably belong to the large hotel nearby.

At Le Rouvraie, the water widens into a great lake and the channel divides. Soon after, as the river turns at 90°, the country is completely open to the right and edged by low wooded hills on the left. It reminds me a little of the canal in Finistère between Carhaix and Châteauneuf, except here the towpath is quite peopled by dog-walkers, old people out strolling and cyclists hurrying along.

At Bocneuf, the towpath moves to the south bank. Again the water is reduced to the merest trickle, presumably for work to be carried out on more gates which look in need of repair. Stagnant water of bilious colour is choked by weed in the channel leading to the lock, which unusually has some pretty willow trees nearby. Further on, a man skilfully operates a digger, hard at work cleaning out the canal bed.

After Lock 42 the Oust comes back in from the right and the canal relishes its fullness once again in a series of beautiful long meanders. To the north of the canal is the Forêt de Lanouée and the village of Les Forges, both once busy sites of Rohan enterprises. The 'garde' in charge of the forest in the mid 15th century was paid 115 deniers a week, a reasonable income with free lodging and firewood thrown in, enough to buy bread and eat meat regularly. This part of the family's estates was especially important for breeding horses, with *haras* (studs) at Branguily and Lanouée. The horses were reared in the wild and then captured as required. Les Forges was the centre of a network of economic activities - wood-cutting, charcoal, metalwork, smithies - connected to the management of the forest.

After passing a large number of goats of all colours and sizes grazing opposite, I reach the start of the feeder canal that leads off to Les Forges. It is signed here like a road junction, and a lovely green avenue of water leads up to the former port. Much of the iron produced at the forges was destined for the arsenal at Brest, and the foundery employed nearly 800 people at the height of its production. Established in the early 17th century by Henri de Rohan, this was an industrial development with political and religious aspects. Masters and workers for the enterprise came from Huguenot metallurgy centres in Maine and Normandy, and a chapel was built to cater for the protestant faith of the community.

Taking in this area at walking pace continually prompts an awareness of the huge web of dependence and patronage centred on the Rohan family, its net creeping out over much of medieval Brittany. That was, of course, a less complex time, when identity was determined by social status, long before the dawn of individualism that has brought us all potentially under the strain of modern identity crises. The Duc de Rohan today in his château must have a profound sense of his ties with the land and its history for good and ill. I do not imagine he wastes a lot of time in wondering where he fits into the overall scheme of things. I begin to realize the extent to which whole lives could be shaped by family identity, with all its weight of duty and responsibility, intensified by the passing of generations and the mercurial demands of history. Far from being suppressed, individualism perhaps has an easier run on that scale of size and importance of family. The name conjures up a powerful apparition of achievement and values, a primed canvas for separate members to contribute their own colourful splashes.

The Rohans placed the greatest possible emphasis on lineage, on the family identity that transmitted their image to the outside world and fuelled their own fervent ambitions and sense of superiority. In the melting pot of nationalities active in medieval Brittany, when Breton identity was severely diluted by noble families turning to the language and culture of the French court for reasons of political expediency, the Rohan clan somehow managed to hang on to their distinctive role, even precariously claiming descent from the ancient Breton kings from the line of Conan Meriadec, legendary leader in Brittany after the departure of the Roman administration. Some also say it was a Rohan who killed Tristan in the Arthurian legend cycle.

I envy anyone with a strong sense of family identity, and find it commoner here in Brittany than elsewhere, another reference to the strong traditional Catholic community. This is something lacking in my own background, with a failure to forge the bonds of parent/child/sibling connection that evolve so naturally for some. The lack of acceptance within my own family had the gravest consequences for my early adulthood, when I had to cling to substitute groups, to school, to sports teams, to university, to learned societies in avoidance of the exposed personality of the more intimate unit. From the reflection on this trip, at last I think I'm evolving beyond those needs and fears, inching as the towpath unfolds mile after mile towards a resolution of an enigma.

I come back to finish this section of walking in sharp, cold weather as winter approaches.

Returning to the north bank at Lock 45, Griffet, the towpath edges wide open fields whilst across the water are poplars bearing great balls of mistletoe. Just up ahead there is a barrier and *route barrée* sign. I decide to ignore it and press on regardless. At a section of red mud where diggers have been working, I see a single deep male footprint - mysterious - and puzzle over it for a while until I deduce that the operator must have put one foot down from the cab and then changed his mind. About a kilometre ahead many men are working around a lock, which is all fenced off, but no-one seems to mind me passing through. The Oust has departed again, leaving the canal bed in its empty *chômage* mode.

It is very quiet once the works are left behind. A seemingly endless straight line of canal rolls out ahead. I stop to eat sandwiches on the tow-path, sitting on a stone marker. The water is absolutely still, with patches of ice here and there. As I sit in quiet contentment, the bells from the Abbey of Timadeuc ring out, the peals sharp in the cold clarity of the air. A sign on the bridge ahead points the way to this 19th century Trappist foundation, which accepts those seeking a few days of religious retreat or attendance at some services. It also makes and sells very good cheese.

M. Cayot Délandre, during an exploration of Morbihan's history and monuments in 1847, visited the Abbey and was profoundly impressed by the singing of the monks. 'The chant of 16 monks, full of richness and devout melody reached me. It was at once both harmonious and serious, with a melancholic charm which penetrated the soul and lifted one from the earth.' What would be the effect, he asked himself, of a hundred voices raised in this way - surely even the most rebellious spirits would be touched and open themselves to religious fervour?

Beyond the lock of Timadeuc there is no ice on the surface of the canal and it feels as if I have suddenly entered a more temperate zone. Here the water is rippling and alive in its movement. I have both my dogs with me today and let them go ahead, hanging back to watch the reflection of the thin trunks opposite in the water like sticks of early asparagus.

The sun comes out between cloudy spells and brief bursts of rain. Here the tow-path is raised like a causeway between the canal on one side and a swampy marshland on the other. The great balls of mistletoe hang from high branches like green chandeliers. Although it is very quiet, this is no wild place. Managed land stretches along the opposite bank, large fields and buildings perched on the hill-top. Farming in this broad valley is large-scale. Occasional flashes of noise from machinery puncture the crisp veil of air and echo among the trees along the water. On nearing Rohan, a most beautiful row of beeches, in winter mode, line the path, and a robin flits sharply enough to attract my attention and let me know he's there, then sits on a branch to watch us go by with a typical robin's healthy curiosity about human activity.

The noise of traffic begins to penetrate my carapace of quiet and, after another graceful sweeping bend, there comes the first sight of the industrial zone that heralds the approach to Rohan. Ahead is a large foaming fall of river whilst the water in the lock beside it, separated only by a slim finger of bank, is absolutely calm, with the stillness of death. The contrast is striking and delineates a metaphor for the canal in its dual guises: action, movement and life alongside inactivity, paralysis and stagnation.

The yellow flags of a Renault garage flutter in what little

breeze is stirring. Soon cars are racing along just above my head on the D2. The river swings to the left then back to widen in front of an attractive old warehouse of mellowed stone. There is another lock here where the former port would have been, and the old three arch stone bridge has been replaced by a modern one. On the right bank stands the beautiful Chapelle de Bon-Encontre, built in 1510 by Jean de Rohan on the site of an earlier church. It bears the Rohan arms, and a picture of Notre-Dame du Rosaire features a crowd with individual faces from the famous family. There is little sign of the Rohan castle, which once stood here before the bridge with its feet in the water, except a large nearby mural giving a romantic glimpse of the town in its glory days.

Next day I am quickly out of Rohan. A man on a bike slows down to say with a delighted nod *'il écoute bien sa patronne!'* of Brian, who sits patiently to command on the appearance of any cyclist. Our smiling exchange takes me out of brooding thoughts about the Rohans and their sense of family identity. I've come to realise that an important lack in my life has been the security of knowledge deriving from a strong link with one's origins, the land where one grew up. I compare my poverty in this context with that of Breton friends whose solid strength of personality derives from the connection with their native environment. Once established, this root cannot be destroyed, but if you fail to set it early on, it is ever harder to force down into passing soil. I was never attached to the small Gloucestershire village and tame landscape I grew up in, and felt a profound relief on leaving it behind. One glimpse of the Brecon Beacons, however, was enough to lift my heart on old journeys to Swansea via the Head of the Valleys route.

Church clocks on each side of the water strike ten at different times, their chimes slightly muffled by the moist air. There is a steep rise to Lock 55, Coet-Prat, where I rest and admire the pretty garden. The towpath moves back to the north bank here and the Oust finally leaves the canal to wend its own way: a veritable close procession of locks is now required to lift the artificial channel up and over into the Blavet valley, passing through the idyllic Forêt de Branguily. After a 90° bend beyond No. 56, the locks come in such rapid sequence that they merge into each other in my memory. The 20kms from Gueltas to Pontivy has 53 locks, up and down, mini reservoirs in between to keep up the water supply.

It is a green and pleasant walk through this forest in any weather, a place to linger and wonder at the engineering feats and powers of endurance of all those who built the canal. This 5 kilometre section, raising the canal from 68m to a height of 129m, was fed by the Rigole d'Hilvern, which brought water from a reservoir at Bosméléac an incredible 63 kilometres away via the contours of the land. Begun in 1824 this feeder stream took fourteen years to construct satisfactorily – the earliest attempts leaked so badly that little water was left at the end of the *rigole*'s serpentine journey. Twenty-four locks mark the extent of this remarkable change in the canal's level up to the Hilvern watershed – another twenty-nine, including a 'ladder' of twelve within 1.6kms near Le Roz, were needed for the descent to Pontivy.

Birds skim like stones along the surface of the water, as the trees get denser. A lost world atmosphere through the peaceful beauty of this deep forest is heightened by ruined lockhouses, with their roofs eaten away and buckling walls, and a sign to the ominously named '*Puits d'Enfer*' or Wells of Hell. The press of greenery squeezes out noise, and I am sorry to return to a world of well-kept houses as the high-point is finally reached at a level of 129m in a sombre channel, the water almost black.

Unfortunately I can no longer ignore a sharp pain in one shin which is making progress increasingly difficult. A busy road is running alongside now, but I nevertheless take willing advantage of a seat, lying down and looking up through the bright leaves at a blue sky. When I try to resume my walk, an excruciating stabbing jolt brings tears to my eyes. I have no choice but to go on.

Fortunately I am distracted by a chance conversation struck

up with 'King' Arthur Spinks, who has lived canalside for 15 years, and whose engaging character and spontaneous offer of hospitality leads to a welcome pause and refreshment. He tells me how the previous owner used to fish for pike from the doorway of his house.

Limping on, I reach another chain of locks which are too close together to merit individual lock-houses. The towpath crosses back to the south side at No.87, a long straight stretch ahead in full sunshine before the last close-stepped descent towards Pontivy, where the first lock is flying the Breton flag. Even against the pain I can appreciate the beautiful scene of water dappled in sunlight as the canal moves steadily towards the Blavet in a wide green decline.

The last 6kms of the day prove something of an endurance test, but turning south towards Pontivy, there is the succour of a particularly lovely tall-treed stretch. I notice one huge red, white-warted toadstool lurking among the roots. Roads are now in earshot as the town gets nearer and many cyclists and dog-walkers people the route towards urban civilisation. It takes all my concentration and mental discipline to keep going: in the face of what feels like red-hot jabs at each step, I creep along like a snail. This is my first experience of what I'm later told is shin-splints. Coming into the town I am only vaguely aware of a neat lock-house and people on the pavements as I struggle to the parking area. Oddly the malady fades away to nothing as soon as I sit down and take my boots off. It must be the strain of accumulated walking after a period of intense activity.

Pontivy is said to have been founded by the monk Ivy in the 7th century. An early château was destroyed in the 14th century and replaced in 1485 by the Rohan foundation which is open to the public today. The medieval streets around the castle contrast with the Napoleonic developments elsewhere in the town which feature huge parade-ground sized squares, barracks and administrative buildings. The town was boosted by the regime at that time as a strategic base in Morbihan against the activities of the anti-revolutionary,

Catholic and monarchist Chouans. Its name changed to Napoléonville at various points in the 19th century (some of the canal bournes had this name inscribed) in a clear example of projected identity through labelling, a practice that applies as much to politics as to breakfast cereal. But Napoleon's legacy of conformity and set standards of French identity were ever at odds with strong notions of regional identity and individuality such as those so apparent in Brittany.

Like Redon, Pontivy is a canal crossroads, with the Blavet providing a link to Hennebont for the arsenal at Lorient on the south coast. The towpath on the Nantes-Brest canal swings north without need to enter the town proper, which I've visited many times before, and on my next trip, I am soon past the sports grounds and cascade where a troop of young people are exercising reluctantly, and away from a brief urban interlude of noise, people and traffic.

From Pontivy to Lac de Guerlédan, the canal stretches mournfully through a flat, uninspiring terrain, its desultory aspect perhaps more apparent here than anywhere else. Symbols of sadness proliferate: rotten lock-gates, water choked by weeds and reeds, indecipherable bournes and enough derelict buildings to suggest mass desertion.

The weather is appalling as I start but rain often sets off the canal to surprising advantage, in the patterns on the water, the damp air and an enhanced greenness in the dripping foliage. In fact, it lends an air of romantic melancholy to some scenes today that might be attractive in the somewhat neglected gardens of a stately home. The canal's identity, however, is bound up in utilitarianism: faded apathy does not suit its spirit. This section really is going nowhere. Here one can feel intensely the contrast between this pathetic invalid and its strong convalescent cousin in Finistère. A reminder of that bright slogan, popular in the 1990s, 'use it or lose it' - good advice for the body, the brain and canals.

In contrast to the weather, I feel good, and delighted to be back on the canal track after all the undulating hill walking I've been doing lately in the Monts d'Arrée. It seems oddly different to be walking consistently south/north, as the Blavet wends its way up towards Lac de Guerlédan.

I soon have to stop to put on waterproofs reluctantly as the rain gets heavy. A graceful line of beeches provides shady arches over the towpath, which is gravel and tarmac for most of the way. My footsteps crunch loudly in the quietness, an echo magnified in the dank atmosphere. A signpost on the towpath points off towards the Chapel de Carme. It's worth the 350m walk (if it's open) to see the 18th century ceiling paintings and those from the 15th century uncovered beneath them during restoration. The chapel benefited, like so much else round here, from the patronage of the Rohans.

The lock at Tréscle is in a bad state. The gates are overgrown by weeds and water gushes through large cracks in the fabric. A ruined building nearby adds to the sense of desolation. A little further on, by contrast, a large private house on the opposite bank has well-kept grounds sweeping down to the water, and a green ladder for swimming access. Hardly necessary today, when wetness is inevitable, but I can see the attraction on a hot day.

This is the end of the peaceful part. From here on there are any number of cars, lorries, vans, farm machinery and noisy agro-industrial premises around the canal to make focused thought and concentration almost impossible. You have to listen very, very carefully to hear the canal sighing. There aren't any people though: apart from two cyclists, I see no other canal users today.

The unremarkable landscape of this shallow valley gradually becomes more visible as the rain clouds lift: occasional low hills on one side or the other, a wind farm, a fishing lake. Nothing to provide a dramatic stage for the canal, nothing to provide the dense privacy that is so often the privilege of canal walking. Where the opposite bank is clear of trees the north-west wind whistles across the water, almost lifting my rain-hat off. Vast areas of grazing land proliferate. I have seen and heard more cows today than ever before in Brittany. The low banks of their pastures here dissolve on the water's edge into muddy little beaches, very like the conditions on the Somerset Levels.

At Le Stumo the river splits around an ancient mill-house with attendant mill-race by the road bridge. It's a handsome stone building, enlivened by a bright display of terraced plants in pots and containers of varied shapes and sizes. Not a natural garden, perhaps, but aesthetically pleasing by virtue of the thought and care that's gone into it. This is in marked contrast to the state of the canal - and little love went into its construction, after all - although near here is the first legible bourne. Unfortunately that's because someone has 'thoughtfully' stuck metal numbers on the old time-eaten stone and used paint to pick out the lettering.

More abandoned lock-houses litter the route, engulfed by vegetation, closed and shuttered in the static grip of lost chances. The lack of people, which I so often regard as a plus, begins to seem a clear factor in the lifelessness of this part of the canal. At Quénécan, the grass round the lock is neatly cut, whilst the lock itself is totally bunged up with weeds. At another lock, the Blavet diverges from the canal, which sinks into an even sorrier state, silted up with scum and weeds as far as the eye can see.

Eventually the barrage before Lac de Guerlédan looms ahead. It is grey and forbidding, like a concentration camp with its high metal gates and huge stark lettering: ELECTRICITE DE FRANCE. In a blink of the eye I go back fifteen years and stand again before the entrance to Auschwitz and the chilling words ARBEIT MACHT FREI. This is not a memory I usually dwell on, but it surges up here, triggered by some faint similarity of building fabric, some lingering trough of despondency. Here in the safe centre of Brittany I remember that time in the Polish countryside, the one day of my life when it seemed too unbearably trivial to listen to Mozart.

But now there's only the hum of the hydraulic station for accompaniment. The sun deigns to shine as I leave the burial ground of the canal to retrace my steps, cross the bridge and tread wearily down the wooded path to St-Aignan. Other commitments are now to intervene and I must break my journey along the canal until the spring.

Chapter 7   Death of a Canal

"I have walked myself into my best thoughts and I know of no thought so burdensome that one cannot walk away from it"
Soren Kierkegaard

The waters of the lake are smooth and inviting. A group of children under instruction yell and shriek in their bright kayaks, the sound echoing up through the evergreens. Lac de Guerlédan, a beautiful spot, a fine leisure resource. But this peaceful lake killed the canal. Beneath its waters are the remains of locks and lock-houses, lost to the world when the valley was submerged in the 1920s, the old blue road drowned by a mightier demand - 'houille blanche', the white oil, electricity. If ever anything died from an electric shock it was the canal, its hopes drowned, promises of a life-line reneged upon, leaving a great severed snake, unable to reconnect its extremities.

This work of destruction began in 1923, with permission for the SGE (Société générale d'entreprise) to manage the canal between Bon Repos and Guerlédan. Twelve kilometres of the Blavet valley were flooded and the lake engulfed 400 hectares of woodland, houses, locks and lock-keepers cottages. The original concept of a ladder of locks to keep through navigation feasible was never realized: canal trade was not great enough to justify the cost. Protests by the *bateliers* (bargemen), for whom a way of living died before their eyes, went unheeded. In September 1930 the barrage and hydro-electric station were opened. Murder in the cold light of day. And the coup de grâce? The electricity fuelled the railway that came along to kick the corpse of the canal in its death throes.

The barrage remains an impressive engineering feat: 206 metres long, 45m high. 50,000,000 cubic metres of water fill the lake. Every ten years it is drained to allow inspection and maintenance. Then the ghostly silhouettes of unfulfilled lives emerge to haunt the memories of the faithful. A ruined house, a rotting lock - empty relics, full of spirits.

So I pick up my canal walking on a warm spring day at the Barrage de Guerlédan. Here walkers have to make decisions about getting round the lake. To the north lie the options of the GR341N or the route of the old metre gauge railway from Carhaix to St-Méen-le-Grand, part of the *Réseau Breton*. Both will eventually lead to Gouarec, but neither is as atmospheric as the southern route through the Forêt de Quénécan, with its connection to the legend of Conomor.

This 6th century historical figure, who as Comte de Poher, the area around Carhaix, played a significant role in the development of early Brittany, also evolved into a folktale bluebeard. Stories of wives buried in the cellar and ruthless violence against rivals have clung to Conomor's memory like sticky-burs. A 700m detour from the barrage car-park will lead to the chapel of Ste-Tréphine (and an easier path above the forest, if required). Tréphine, his young second wife, was decapitated by her husband when pregnant to avoid fulfillment of the prophecy that his son would kill him. Saint Gildas intervened to bring Tréphine back to life, but years later Conomor did succeed in killing Trémeur, the young boy she bore. A stained glass window in the church of Pédernec (just west of Guingamp) graphically depicts the defiant Conomor's excommunication for misdeeds by a council of nobles and bishops on the hill of Menez Bré.

A little way along the demanding lakeside route GR341S, a springy path on which I seem to bounce along the forest floor, the outcrop of Kastell Finans, strategic stronghold of Conomor, rises above the lake. Perfectly positioned for protecting the boundary with the pre-Roman Coriosolites' tribal frontier, it provided a tough base for defending the Poher and Conomor's mineral resources, the gold of the Blavet, and lead-silver mines of Poullaouen.

Despite the natural beauty of the track through the forest, the bird-song - especially the deafening shout of cuckoos - and spring flowers, there's something a touch melancholic in the air. The vast valley feels completely empty: a suspense of time and motion, as nothing touches the glaucous waters of the lake. It's a sort of grey-green day that matches my mood, dull water glimpsed through spring green leaves. Down by the lake, lulled by the gentle plash of water on the over-hanging trees, a slick of yellow pollution lines the shore for miles. It looks like paint or a particularly revolting soup.

There has been little sign of activity on the water so far, but by the time I reach the Anse de Sordan, things are livelier. A couple of motor boats carve up the water at high speed, their arrogant swell rocking a few quiet fishing vessels, and a pleasure-boat passes, full of sightseers out from Beau Rivage on the opposite shore. On land, there are children cavorting in the playground and an English family having a picnic.

After lunch, the sun appears and it gets hot very quickly. The lake is narrowing and rocky outcrops are more and more frequent. I now enter the part of the forest which is off limits in the hunting season. The path traverses a narrow strip of land between the water and a line of tape denoting that the woodland is private property. It's no longer so peaceful, with noisy machinery active in the quarries on the opposite shore.

The path is difficult in places as it undulates along the hillside, dropping to the waterline and then rising steeply again. Much of the time it is necessary to scramble over rocks. I miss a foothold and fall heavily onto my weak left knee. From that point, the track seems interminable. I can see the folds of lake and forest stretching ahead, but such close attention to the ground is needed that much of the pleasure of the surroundings is lost. I'm not carrying unlimited water and the temperature continues to rise together with the effort of the endless ups and downs. Eventually, as I begin to wonder if I will ever escape the clutches of this timeless forest, at the top of a steep rise I find myself looking down on a lock, Ecluse de Belle Vue. The thought of regaining the canal and a level path is enough to send me down that slope at speed.

A short stint of road walking leads to Bon Repos, where Alain de Rohan founded a Cistercian abbey in the 12th century after stopping to rest here and dreaming of the Virgin Mary. The acts of foundation survive, indicating the precision with which such decisions were legally enshrined even in that early era. Alain's wife Constance, daughter of

Conan, Duke of Brittany, and Countess of Richmond in England by virtue of her Penthièvre family holdings, was also associated with him in the documentation. Various lands in Brittany and England were assigned to the new establishment, including Foulbourn near Cambridge.

The ruins of the abbey are currently under restoration, in the care of a local association formed in 1986, and my first view is a renewed version of the 18th century south-east façade originally contributed by a secular abbot. From the lavish style it appears that by then the abbey functioned as his domain rather than a religious building, requiring a degree of grandeur appropriate for the promotion of his own personal image. So the building became a statement of identity, a manifestation of wealth, of taste and contemporary style. It was later partly burnt by the Chouans, and for a time around 1832 housed engineers working on the canalisation of the Blavet.

Inevitably now the abbey has an air of 'management' - as well as exhibitions and accommodation, it hosts spectacular *son et lumière* shows in summer which gallop energetically through snippets of Breton history. I lie on a picnic bench for a while and contemplate the older ruined sections across the water of the Blavet, enjoying the idea of resting in the same spot as Alain de Rohan and absorbing the beauty of the setting.

At last, back to the canal, which I have come to know and love so well. My legs have a new lease of life as I embark on the last five kilometre stretch of the day towards Gouarec. Walking on the south side now, it feels odd to have the water to the right. My stride falls into a natural rhythm and, despite the noise of traffic on the N164, I feel restored and purposeful. Just past the 241km stone, the canal sweeps right, the road disappears and suddenly, peace and green descend, with avenues of trees on both sides and the craggy Landes of Liscuis, with their poignant Neolithic burial places, looming above to the north. A thin, deep lily-padded lake to the left is part of plans to restore the environment for pike and other fish, according to a notice-board. What looks like a turtle or terrapin, about a foot long, breaks the surface and then plunges below the water.

On the approach to Gouarec, the towpath becomes increasingly busy: joggers, strollers, cyclists, dog-walkers all out to enjoy the spring weather in the Bois de Gouarec, all cheerful under the canal's spell. Here it is providing a focus for human activity and the usage is a lifeline, but, as so often, restricted to a few kilometres near a centre of habitation.

Under the D5 road bridge, Breton political slogans in huge blue letters are painted:

FREE BRITTANY. THE PATIENCE OF THE BRETONS IS LIKE THE COMPETENCE OF THE FRENCH ADMINISTRATION: IT HAS ITS LIMITS

This is not the expression of the anarchists of the 1970s with their bombs and missiles, but the terminally frustrated, struggling with intelligence and grim humour against the indifference of their compatriots as well as the on-going torments of their Gallic overlords. It seems these days not so much the desire for political independence as for distinct and discreet identity, a recognition of linguistic and cultural values: an end of the Breton visage disfigured by French surgery.

In the centre of Gouarec, I cross the bridge, follow the other bank of the canal for a few hundred metres and then cut through a camping site to a new passerelle over a backwater. To the left is the welcome sight of my over-night stop, an English-owned B&B, where I am very well looked after with much kindness, good food and a very comfortable room.

Business is not exactly brisk for accommodation providers: the market is pretty saturated by British people hoping to eek out a living by letting rooms or gites. When we leave the next morning I can't help reflecting on the difficult circumstances of many English people living in Brittany, the sadness and disappointment underlying many a story of effort and struggle. I suppose those who are well-settled and contented never expected a new life in a new country to be a panacea for ills that blighted their lives in the UK. Those with holiday homes or who retain a property back in England often seem happier - they are the ones with choices, unlike the unlucky ones cut off from families and constrained by financial considerations from longed-for contact with loved ones. There is a great gulf between those who are here because they want to be and those who are basically economic migrants, lured by the attractions of cheap housing and Brittany's proximity to the UK. But the cheap house is only the start: it's no cheaper to live here, and money is harder to generate. When the capital runs out, making a living is far from easy.

The problems of relationships are often heightened by the pressures of moving abroad and frequently women feel the strain most, isolated from sustaining friendships and easy occupation. The psychological disadvantage of not speaking a language can be immense and the shifting balance of relationships bewildering for one or both partners. He or she who made decisions and got things done in England may not be the one who manages to speak French well enough to maintain that role over here. In addition to the strangeness of daily custom and practice can be added the massive weight of redrawn lines in a marriage or partnership - and this is without any consideration of associated problems such as unhappy children or financial pressures.

It is potentially undermining of personal identity to uproot and start again in a foreign country where different language, custom and habit are unsettling. Familiar social and economic systems, and a network of friends and family ties provide a more comfortable context than we realize until those links are severed or over-stretched.

The delicate human mechanism of coping with change also needs its subtle movements to incorporate the weather (long dark winters seem to take people by surprise), the Breton tendency to stay indoors, to mix with only family and take their time in opening up to outsiders.

Changes of status are even harder to assimilate in another country. Identity is a form of credential, a level of social identification, and how we introduce ourselves is usually instructive. I'm Joe Bloggs, Alice's's husband, I'm Joe Bloggs, from London, I'm Joe Bloggs, I work in computers, and so on. Happy the man who says 'I'm Joe Bloggs' and leaves it at that, who has no need to define himself with reference to externals. This is the truest confidence of identity, because true identity is unspoken. Labouring to define is to betray need for recognition and a certain level of insecurity. When I left a good job in London and moved to Somerset to concentrate on writing, I found it hard to say who I was without the clarity of status attached to work. Always without work I have been much less happy in my life, and I soon realised that my own notions of identity were intimately connected to some sort of creative productivity: perhaps that's why I always intended, from the age of about 7, to write books, for tangible evidence of my existence.

How to live in a foreign country is not just a matter of language lessons and attending the local *fest-noz* - it's an attitude of mind that's needed. There is no shortage of extremes here: those who have no intention whatsoever of learning a word of French (and there are plenty of those with the abhorrent 'English is the international language' sort of attitude), those who only mix with English and utilize the numerous English shops and businesses here - and at the other end of the scale, those who speak French well and shun their un-educated English compatriots as beneath contempt.

Artificial integration is like artificial insemination, anathema to some, life-line to others. It's a complex and often infuriating exercise of trying to balance unequals. I don't want to be patronized by the French any more than I want to befriend every British person I meet in the supermarket. We are not French or Bretons, and never will be: it is as individuals we can each find our own place here and make our own contribution as time and circumstances dictate. It comes as quite a relief to articulate this idea to myself and feel its resonance: maybe I'm really getting somewhere at last.

Today I set off early for a 25 kilometre stint to Glomel. It starts off grey and overcast, later alternating between very fine drizzle and bursts of hot sunshine emerging from black clouds. Some pretty wiggles of the canal lead out of Gouarec before the towpath crosses to the north bank at Lock 142, Pleulaff. All is quiet: buttercups along the bank, the obligatory single fisherman on each lock, decoratively placed like gnomes on a garden pond. Locks are increasingly frequent as the canal begins its long climb to the highest point of 184 metres, where the connection between the Blavet and the Aulne valley will be effected by the Bief de Glomel. At Coat-Nautous is the only double lock (No.146) along the entire length of the canal.

From this point is one of the most beautiful sections of the whole route from Nantes to Brest. Across a large lake beyond the lock is the Chapelle de la Pitié with its stone fontaine nearby. A picturesque scene, but it's the natural beauties ahead that bring a new sense of peace and fulfilment. There's a change in the atmosphere, the quality of air, of sound, of the water's gentle flow. It's odd how one type of bird seems to dominate at any given time: today the woodpeckers are furiously and noisily active in the trees across the water. Here the birds don't need to compete with the traffic on the N164 as they seem to do on other stretches, their song resonating with the utmost clarity between strips of woodland.

May and a late spring are perfect for wildflowers, which burgeon along the banks and verges. Yellow irises at the water-line, bluebells in the woods, vetch, speedwells, celandines, orchids, swathes of borage, viper's bugloss and an occasional clover decorate the verges. There's a general sense of activity and movement in the banks and run-off slicks of stagnant water. A mother mallard hides her chicks under over-hanging branches as I stride by, wagtails dip and bob over the water and a great buzzard flies out of a copse at head height making me jump, and powers away up in a great soaring circle before settling on the highest branch of a very tall tree on the opposite bank.

The canal continues to climb with each lock and they begin to merge into each other in my mind. No.147, a pretty house with buddleia in full bloom and roses around the door, is clearly owned by someone who loves plants in a natural, wild way, not the manicured form I've seen at so many lock-houses along the earlier route. There are bright blue shutters on the un-rendered cottage at Kerisloyet, and a caravan in the garden plastered with Breton symbols. There is little sign of life at any of these houses as I pass, except for a man peering out from behind a net curtain as I stop on a bridge to take photos. Most are shut up, waiting for a brief lease of life during the traditional French vacation month of August.

At this point, the phenomenon so common to my canal walking kicks in - the long thought again, that drawn out thread of reflection that can lead to creative enlightenment or into the darkest corridors of personal dilemma. I'm in the latter now, so deeply immersed in reflections of change that I would not have noticed an otter tap-dancing on the towpath in front of me. My experience of living in Brittany seems to have produced another persona to add to my life-time repertoire, and at the same time the stirring connection to a deeper memory of some former self.

The ribbon of water leads me on, winding out that thought to an excruciating length like some primitive instrument of torture. One is unaccustomed to such quality of thought: it is unique to the canal, where no busyness of water, no whizzing traffic distracts from the focus. Neither is one constrained by the static atmosphere of a study or library nor diverted by a wide view or uneven terrain. That's all there is, the long thought, and for its duration, it can point the way to ecstasy or despair. On the other hand, walking is considerably cheaper than psychotherapy and probably just as efficacious, if for long enough.

I break out of the trap on coming to a sequence of *étangs*, lakes shaped on the map like a series of squeezed balloons with locks at the pinch-points. Here the canal takes on a new character as the towpath continues along the north side, sometimes becoming a causeway between two expanses of water. One to the right has a primeval stillness with smooth dead branches protruding from the black water like monster skeletons. My mind wanders quickly without the focus of the customary strait, as the intrinsic character of the channel is lost and replaced by an alien expansiveness of ruffled wavelets, the wind taking advantage of the openness to raise its stakes.

Half a dozen locks in quick succession have been necessary to bring the water up to this level: the lakes were concomitants to keep up supply for movement of boats through the locks and in the long artificial channel ahead. Across the D3 I am finally at the start of the *bief de partage*, working up to the Grande Tranchée, a great slice more than three kilometres in length cut through the hillside in the 1820s by a workforce consisting mainly of prisoners from the *bagne* in Brest. In order to join the Blavet and Aulne valleys, the canal here reaches its greatest height of 184m above sea-level, and it is sobering to reflect on the effort and sacrifice of health (and often life) required in this achievement.

The workers were housed in a barrack-like camp up the hill to the south of the valley they struggled to create in appalling conditions, the damp and humidity a tempting breeding ground for disease. A hospice in Rostrenen was found for the sick: its records of deaths show that the prisoners came mainly form southern France, and the guards from Brittany. After the 1830 revolution in Paris the prisoners, mainly deserters from the Spanish wars, broke out of the camp and a large group tried to make their way to Pontivy to gain confirmation from officialdom that they now had the right to freedom. They were persuaded to return, but the camp was finally closed in 1832 after a cholera scare, and a fire destroyed much of it not long after.

I pay silent respects to these men as I come level with the former location of the camp, deploring the flippant information boards recounting the story with stupid pictures of a man in striped prison clothing and a ball and chain - what an inappropriate tribute to the men who struggled here under compulsion, their bodies exhausted and often sick, heads filled with dreams of reunions with families far away in unknown circumstances. The Grande Tranchée is a long, lonely stretch with an eerie claustrophobic atmosphere, still tainted by the unrewarded depth of their endeavour and suffering. It remains for me the ultimate symbol of the human cost of building the canal, a memory to be preserved with dignity and without trivialization.

The vista seems to roll away into the distance, getting longer and longer as I walk. This must be an illusion! I feel very tired, nearing the end of a long day's walk. The path is wet and mud splashes up the back of my bare legs with every step. For a minute I indulge in the realization that there are only two more kilometres to cover before a good meal and comfortable bed, but that sense of achievement is laughable in this location where hundreds of men laboured year after year in such horrific conditions to make the canal we see now a reality.

Abruptly after this hypnotic stage the canal opens out into a broad, stagnant lake and the towpath swings round to the first lock in the ladder which will descend towards the Aulne. That's for tomorrow. Now I cross the lock on a footbridge, trudge round the lake and reach Canal Chouette, a superb haven for walkers run by Marie-Jeanne Templier. A walker herself, she understands exactly what's required. There are hot drinks facilities and a large bottle of water in the en-suite room which, like the others in a low wooden extension, overlooks the lake. When I stagger into the *salle* after a good rest, there's an open fire in the modern fireplace, photos and paintings of the canal on the walls and shelves of books on walking and local history, with all the main works on the canal in pride of place.

It's good to talk to someone who shares a passion for the canal and its history. She understands my commitment to this project, demonstrating the strong sense of fellowship to be found among canal aficionados. For many people across Brittany, this waterway is entrenched in their childhood memories, and plays a part in countless personal histories. Like a secret society, you know by the looks exchanged with people on the towpath those who understand where they are and those who pass through heedless. It's like the recognition of potential lovers.

After an excellent meal - delicate potage, robust cassoulet, Breton cake - there is time for browsing and dozing by the fire until sleep seems the only possibility and my romantic fantasies of lying awake thinking through all I've seen during the day prove completely delusional.

The dull, grey skies of the morning turn out to be the best weather of the last day of this trip. The series of locks descends with rectangular basins between each one, like giant's steps. Going downhill and walking at last in the same direction as the flow of the water seems to put me in greater harmony with the canal and the natural direction of things. Yellow irises grow together in great profusion, flowers like velvet sword-hilts, leaves sharp as blades. A reed-bed by the bank is full of large freshwater mussel shells, maybe the remains of feasting by an otter or ragondin. Everything is very quiet again, with no sign of human life, although one boarded up lock-house has a newly dug vegetable patch of very black soil. There is light rain now and the dampness brings out the smell of leaves all around. I sit down for a minute by the bridge at La Pie and enjoy the cheering sight of a weasel flashing across the grass a few metres away. Many small branches litter the towpath as if snapped off in the wind overnight.

In one of those swift weather changes that is a Breton forte, the sun bursts out and lights up the water. With constant movement of shadows and showers of brightness, the whole landscape is alive, peopled by insects and birds, flowers and leaves. By contrast as the canal descends quite steeply, some of the deep locks are neglected and clogged with scummy water. The Moulin de Tronjoly, Lock 84, is a pleasant surprise with fresh painted green woodwork. This is probably a well-walked section, as the GR37 runs along the towpath for some distance here.

At St-Eloy, the corpse of a building is all that remains of the lock-house, now overgrown with ivy, and trees rooted inside its ruined walls. A sad sight, but this whole stretch seems un-maintained and neglected with bushes growing by the waterline up to a height of about four metres so the canal is invisible behind them.

It feels as if few people walk here and, whilst no-one dislikes the taming of nature more than I do, the unkempt banks, overgrown bournes and ruined lock-houses are symbolically pitiful. I hear my footsteps rising and falling in the emptiness, crackling on twigs and stones and fallen blossoms. Crunch, crack, crack as tiny stones rub together.

Home at last! How strongly that sensation comes as I cross into Finistère at Pont Goariva, where the D83 wends south to Plévin. Not far beyond the noisy road, the towpath becomes a causeway between the canal, which turns at 90° and a lake to the right. At once there are navigational signs, an indication that the canal is in use again from here onwards. I have lunch at a picnic table under a group of trees between the two watercourses. There are caterpillars everywhere, falling from the trees into my hair and racing each other across the wooden table, drawing their tiny bodies up into a high arched loop and then propelling themselves forward at a speed dramatic for their size.

The rain comes now, spitting through the wind. I reluctantly put on a waterproof and soldier on uncomfortably, passing the stiff corpse of a frog on his back in the middle of the path. It's strange how the enormity of death can leave no mark. There is an over-powering smell of cut grass as the verges and banks have just been shorn - the three tractors responsible are having a lunch-break on the bank.

This is not a wild stretch of the canal. There are roads and houses in a broad valley with open views. That familiar sense of enclosed loneliness is lost in the open meadows on both sides. A sudden manic and ferociously loud braying indicates the donkey chambres d'hôtes mentioned by Jacques Clouteau in his guide to walking the canal published after he made the trip with his own donkey Ferdinand more than ten years ago.

The rain continues steadily. I'm troubled by a painful tenderness just above my left ankle, a feeling fearfully like that which marred my arrival in Pontivy. There's nothing to see, no blister or bruise, but the lightest rub of my walking boot hurts like hell and I've been limping for the last few kilometres. I take the boot off with difficulty and put an extra sock on that foot. The pain abates for a few hundred metres and then starts again in earnest. A covered seating area near the Pont du Daoulas I had hopes of is fully occupied by a group of cyclists who look well settled in for lunch, so I exchange greetings and move on.

Now begins a phenomenon that is to be relatively common in Finistère: the car on tow-path. The first man deigns to slow down a little as I am reluctant to move into the wet grass and expect him to take the trouble to keep well over. Once past, he revs the engine and shoots off at speed. While I sit on a stone block to rest a little later in the pouring rain, another car comes by very fast along the towpath. The driver looks at me and I manage a very weary smile for politeness' sake. He ignores me completely, maybe correctly reading my mind, which would personally like to slash his tyres or topple the wretched car into the canal.

For the last two kilometres I decide to undo my boot and walk with it open, a blessed relief and remarkably manageable once I adjust to a different sort of step with each foot and the slight roll it gives my gait.

Coming up to the last lock before the end of this journey I'm startled by an extraordinarily loud and strange noise coming from the woods opposite. I capture it on tape but am none the wiser for listening to it later. Is it birds? Machinery? I stop to listen for a couple of minutes, hoping to crack the mystery, but give up defeated. I can only think it was a menagerie of exotic animals all yelling at once in a cacophony of strident screeching.

At last the old industrial mill-buildings of Port de Carhaix loom up. These are mostly ruined and empty, although one is done up handsomely, perhaps as offices and another, a silo, is in noisy operation. I cross the busy main road and then the canal to reach the car-park where a friend is waiting in my car. The transition in speed is strange as I drive north, impatient for the empty heights of the Monts d'Arrée.

Chapter 8 From Hyères to Aulne

"Now shall I walk or shall I ride?
'Ride' Pleasure said: 'Walk' Joy replied."
W.H.Davies

Port de Carhaix must once have been a lively place. It isn't now: the dry toilet by the car-park is about as exciting as it gets. I must find out how this works one day. Otherwise the impression is of decay and neglect among the old industrial buildings. Just over a kilometre up the road is another melancholy sight, the Calvaire de Kerbreudeur, one of the oldest in the area, dating from 1450-1475, a little forlorn now, on a roadside bank as traffic whizzes by, oblivious to its sculptural merits.

It's a public holiday in France. I'm walking westwards on the edge of Finistère, accompanied by Brian the dog. The day does not begin auspiciously. I set out past the *pepinières*, attuning myself to shut out the noise of cars rushing past on the main D769. Mist is rising from the water and, as so often, the spell of the canal starts to draw me away from everyday preoccupations to long mental sweeps of connection, stretching ahead into the future, replacing the little choppy snatches of thought produced by travel among a host of cars.

Then suddenly a van is hurtling towards me along the towpath, splashing up water crudely from the puddles. A most unwelcome surprise, but I get out of the way and hold onto Brian, giving a friendly nod to the driver which is barely acknowledged by the sour-faced man who passes. He clearly thinks he has more right here than I do. It's another manifestation of that modern arrogant assumption that driving is more important than walking. But who does the canal belong to after all? Its original purpose was the transport of goods, so the tow-path provided a track for horses to draw the barges. Its current existence as a leisure resource suggests that walkers and cyclists should have priority, but wheeled vehicles seem alarmingly common.

Access for houses, fishing spots, maintenance is necessary but I suspect some of the older people are just out for a drive on a safe route as long as their steering and concentration are good. Naturally I believe the canal path belongs most to walkers, who echo the slow steady pace of the horses and hopefully don't leave as much ordure along the way. That a speeding bike is no way to enjoy the canal, just an easy and routine form of exercise, is becoming my refrain.

Another vehicle, this time behind me, comes up just as fast, a 4-track from its loud clumsiness. Another miserable driver who gives the sort of nod common to his breed that is barely visible to the naked eye. It's impossible to settle down again and stop holding myself alert for more wheeled traffic without respect for anything less than a 480bhp engine. I was right, the same car comes back the other way minutes later - it's like walking along a road.

I complain bitterly to the canal, which isn't very responsive, holding onto its secrets, cool, glassy and sphinx-like in expression. We join the Hyères, coming in from the right. There's an up-and-down wooden bridge that makes me think of Japanese gardens, although nothing could have less in common with the rich countryside I'm entering. Attached though I am to the deserted wastes of the Monts d'Arrée, this green heart of Finistère is a telling contrast, with nature always well-advanced compared with my home territory a little further north.

Crossing by the lock at Koz Kastell (the old castle), the tow-path accommodates the GR37 for a bit before the long-distance footpath swings off north towards Huelgoat and the Monts d'Arrée. The water of the Hyères is fast-flowing here. There is a path on the other bank, presumably providing access for fishermen or maintenance - a grassy track unlike the made-up tarmac road I'm on and I want to be over there. (In fact, I discover later it's an old railway line, part of the Réseau Breton linking Carhaix with Camaret.) The other side of the canal always has a special allure, frequently of wildness and inaccessibility. The tameness of tow-path walking occasionally makes one long to be thrashing a way through virgin territory along the water-line opposite. The reality is not so pleasant, however, as I once discovered when taking a guided walk at Châteauneuf-du-Faou and finding half-way round that the canal had flooded and our path was under water, forcing a trek through undergrowth along the steep bank above.

The water beside me is talking, as it bubbles round the banks of huge slabs of slate. The sound of water would be a good subject for a book, if the author was a poet rather than some scientist who'll stand about on bridges with an audiometer and ultrasonic devices noting figures and failing to open his own ears. Even the canal has the musical range of a large orchestra, and an endless variety of silence.

I'm now entering a space of deep, anticipatory hush, as if the world has fallen silent before the entrance of an immortal presence. I can hear this silence now and almost feel the looming appearance of some unseen entity. Who are the gods of the canal? I imagine a huge, rather green skinned, weed-draped figure rising out of the centre of the water to give me advice, like the god of the river Tiber looming up to tell Aeneas that a sow and her piglets will mark the spot where Rome will one day stand. The guardian spirits of the canal here must be grey creatures of the slate that forms the bedrock of the whole structure.

Construction of the canal in Finistère began with the first lock at Port-Launay in 1811, opened with fanfares as a monument to the glory and grandeur of Napoleon. (Three years later the same municipal council revelled in his decline.) The short stretch back to Châteaulin was completed over the next 15 years. Mostly local labour was employed in this part of Brittany, overseen by entrepreneurs from Brest, and the work provided kept down the numbers of those leaving the countryside for the towns or abroad in the early part of the 19th century. From 1822 to 1828 work continued eastwards towards Pont-Pol near St-Thois and then to the junction with the Hyères at Pont Triffen. Canalisation of the 10km section of the Hyères took place between 1824 and 1834 so that the whole Finistère route was open in October of that year. Needs of the port at Port-Launay later dictated the destruction of its lock, to be replaced by the last of the canal just downstream at Guily-Glas. This was inaugurated by Napoleon III and the Empress Eugene in 1858.

The canalized might of the magnificent Aulne follows a series of huge loops and bends over more than 60kms to Guily-Glas (the Green Grove), more than double the distance of a fairly straight road between the two points. Such an exceptionally cursive flow is common to rivers passing through this sort of terrain where the channel cuts through banks of schist, but it made the journey time for movement of goods a slow one, one reason why mercantile business was never especially brisk. In winter parts of the canal were non-navigable in bad weather, introducing a further element of unreliability. The canal has always suffered from the piecemeal sort of management that is still a factor today. In general organization of the canal network in Brittany was poor, and many boats travelled empty or only half-full for long distances.

Transport of commodities reached its heyday between 1880 and 1914. Slate, lime, fertilizer, wood, cereals and charcoal were the major cargoes. Grain - the characteristic blé noir (buckwheat), oats and rye - went east to Nantes and from there also on to Bordeaux. Back from Nantes came salt, coffee, oil, sugar and wine. Wood was required not only for domestic use and to fuel bakers' ovens, but also for construction and naval yards, such as those at Port-Launay and Brest, and for pit-props in south Wales. But the two main industrial cargoes were slate and fertilizers. The importance of the latter for areas of poor soil was crucial and the canal was the main method of distribution in central Finistère.

This is a very warm and sunny day. I'm too hot, even in T-shirt and cotton trousers and wish I'd worn shorts. The flow of water is now slowing and I do too, wondering if my pace automatically adjusts to match that of the canal or if it's just that my pack is getting heavy? I seem to have marched along the stretch of faster flowing water more quickly than along the slow bits where most movement is below the surface.

I'm thinking about an approaching visit to England, and the strangeness of revisiting what was once so familiar and now seems so remote. I am feeling that it would take me a long time to re-integrate into English life and then I remember that I never managed it in the first 45 years of my life either. The question of integration seems to be a popular one here in Brittany but it is as complex as the issue of identity, with which it is intimately linked. Many set the bar at the level of language, but I don't believe speaking good French is the key to a happy life in Brittany. I know from observation and experience that individuals who are content with themselves and open to others will find their place anywhere. Bonds of significant friendship develop between neighbours who share only a few words of each other's language. He who raises the question of integration or identity, or makes an issue of these abstracts, is effectively often making a declaration of insecurity and an inverted plea for the sort of acceptance that has not come naturally. I have enjoyed evenings of stimulating conversation and warm personal exchange through a mixture of English, Breton and French - sometimes in the same sentence - but immediately understandable. This is communication, a sharing of ideas, thoughts and feelings, something positive, harmonious and basically joyful between individuals across 'identity boundaries' of nationality and language.

I'm enjoying being on familiar territory in this Finistère stretch of the canal: the landscape is well-known and very important to me, so it is like walking with a friend in a compelling silence broken only by birdsong echoing from the wooded hill-sides. That is, until another wretched car breaks the spell, coming very fast along the path behind me, round a bend. Brian is running free ahead. I call to him to wait and then go - without undue hurry - to hold him. Another sullen, silent man glares at me. I've held him up for all of seven seconds. How strange that in a couple of hours I've seen no walkers or cyclists, only these annoying men in cars.

But seeing houses across the fields as I round a bend, I

realize this is a road to somewhere as well as being a towpath, and people live along it. The towpath has to be many things to many people these days: isolationism is not an option for the modern canal. At the next lock, the lock-keeper's cottage, which is pretty and well-kept, has an English car and a French car outside. I envy them their location on this very beautiful section with little sense of roads or people, if only I can put my unlucky four-wheeled encounters aside. Kilometre stones are interspersed with lumps of concrete providing an opportunity for sitting in the sun. This winding stretch of canal provides enticing changes of perspective, the curving lines of trees with their bright leaves undulating in shifting patterns of sunlight and shadow. Past La Gare, the land opens up, red cattle graze in the meadows unfazed by a sound like gunfire a little distance away beyond the woods. My first real human encounter of the day is sharing a special sight with two other walkers coming towards me. We all stop to watch a heron rise from the bank, glide unhurriedly across the river and perch on the top of a tree. The mutual experience brings warm greetings and smiles. I move on through a veritable crowd of butterflies: could any other part of the canal be as beautiful as this?

Arrival at Pont-Triffen, where there is now a seasonal information centre, the Maison du Canal, in the former lockhouse, brings the modern world of speed and noise firmly back as the N164 runs close to the canal for a few kilometres. This is truly a centre of communications, with the motorway, the former railway and the sweep of the Aulne from the north to take over the business of the canal from the Hyères, like a resolute older sibling. A warbler in the gorse bushes between canal and road holds its own against the harsh continuo of traffic as the sun goes behind clouds.

Young people are out and about, some fishing, their mopeds cast carelessly aside on the bank, and further along, a couple kissing behind a tree on the towpath, embarrassed by my sudden appearance and Brian's interest. Once the canal swings south towards Lock Rosgohuen, peace descends again and suddenly the sun shines through the pine trees onto the water in one of those complete transformations the canal does so well. The Aulne runs wide and fast now beyond the weir and another pretty lock-cottage. These huge sweeping bends, sheened with light silvery in its brightness on the river, make for a majestic sight, the great broad mass of water like a Breton Amazon. A long straight vista and final gentle bend bring me to Pont du Stang where the day's journey ends.

Early one morning some days later, I pick up the Finistère trail. The first hint of summer is here and one of my favourite smells, freshly mown-grass fills the air. Just to the right of the towpath is a little lake with weeping willow, a pretty sight on this clear and still morning. Some dog mimicking the howl of a wolf starts up high above the opposite bank, the sound echoing across the valley as noises routinely reverberate in the channel of the canal.

It's good to be back on the towpath, getting into a rhythm, watching the water, listening to birds and the receding sound of traffic. To my right are open farmland and a low hill crowned with agricultural buildings; to the left a steep bank with tall deciduous trees. The last few days have been so warm that the canal waters look soft and lazy, but with a dense brown tinge, so not totally inviting for swimming. Yellow irises are everywhere and large daisies open their eyes wide on the bank. As so often there is a contrast between the two sides of canal: sunny grassy grazing land dotted with cows and tall, dense, dark, cool woodland right down to the water. There are a couple of horses on the opposite towpath, and I glimpse blue fabric of what must be a tent. Up ahead to the south I can see the densely wooded hill range of the Montagnes Noires, which possibly got their name from this natural feature or from the dark slate concealed in their slopes.

At the Ecluse de Gwaker, which is a *gîte de groupe*, people are sitting outside at tables. The only one to greet me, or rather my dog, is a small white terrier who tags along behind and shows not the least desire to return to its home or owner.

Brian gets used to it and they start playing, their antics distracting, amusing and annoying by turns. If I had known this was to go on for 4 kilometres I might have taken sterner action at the start. Still, the birds seem undisturbed by canine grunts and yaps. My romantic impression of the total freedom of the aviarian life is nonsense, of course. Birds are constrained by rituals and seasonal needs, but what makes them hop from one branch to another? Is it a decision, a plan, an instinct - why here and not there?

A heron flies along low over the water and then stops on the bank ahead. There is another not far off. Dragon-flies dart everywhere. I revel in the quiet and the shade of tall, capacious oak trees along this route.

The lock of Le Moustoir has a wonderful setting in wild woodland. From here there is a long path up to the 16th century chapel of the same name which I remember has pretty gardens and a simple calvaire I found very moving on my first visit.

Brian has grown tired of his assiduous companion and wants to be left alone. I've tried shouting and pretending to throw stones, but it's impossible to fool a terrier. I begin to think I'll have to go to the mairie in Châteauneuf and persuade them to ring the lock and get someone to collect the dog. Again, I am stupidly ignoring the intelligence of this type of dog, something I should know well enough from childhood pets and helping out in kennels and rescue centres back in England.

The river turns sharply to the left this time. The countryside is mostly wooded, with a vertical hillside by the towpath. Foxgloves are out all along the bank, the dance of the dragonflies continues, all is very green and lush. The sun reignites fiercely, although it is not yet mid-morning, so that my face feels hot and red. Despite the exceptional verdure and natural tranquillity of this part of the canal, it is also an area with heavy reminders of the harsh economic realities of life in which it played its part. The land I can see opposite is that of the commune of St-Goazec, where the first quarries were exploited as early as 1486.

One result of constructing the canal in Finistère in the 19th century was a rapid growth in slate quarries along its length, with this material much in demand for roofing and facing houses. Quimper cathedral and the Chapel des Invalides in Paris were notable buildings covered with Breton slate. Direct transport to Port-Launay made these enterprises an economic reality for a time: from there, slate was transported all around the north coast of Brittany. Quarries were to be found in the communes of Châteaulin, Lopérec, Saint-Coulitz, Pleyben, Lothey, Gouézec, Lennon, Spézet, Motreff, Châteauneuf and Saint-Goazec. All except seven of these were open to the sky and most were near the canal. They were mainly small enterprises, not lucrative enough to invest in modern machinery to aid the extraction.

The remains of the best known, the Ardoisières du Rick or Rick Quarry, are now coming into sight across the canal, a great expanse of open slate on the very steep hillside opposite. As I move towards this, the water is stagnant after flowing so freely further upstream. Grass from verge-cutting has blown into the canal and been drawn out by the under-current into a long thread like an Andy Goldsworthy creation. There is a shimmer of dust in the air - whilst each side of it remains oddly crystal-clear - in one localized spot near the mined hillside, as if to draw attention to its past significance.

This small enterprise was taken over and expanded by Count Louis de Kerjegu, (uncle of the founder of the Château de Trévarez) at the end of the 19th century. Constructed at the top of the left bank at Saint-Goazec, the premises never flooded, unlike many others. The quarry was 80 metres deep, too deep for men to carry out the slate without aid, so the slog of shifting it up to the surface was helped by trucks on conveyor-belts, a refinement not enjoyed by most other establishments where workers at the quarry face (*au fond*) were required not only to tolerate the danger of rock falls, but also to hump great weights on their backs to the surface. The blocks of schist went to the lines of little cabin workshops, where the *fendeurs* - better paid for their skills - bent over double much of the day, split and shaped them into slates.

106

Quarrying was horrendously hard toil. Accidents and occupational illnesses claimed many lives. Bronchitis and tuberculosis were common, and few in that line of work reached retirement age. A medical report described the norm: 'after twenty years, they have difficulty breathing, breathless at the least effort, their chest whistling, coughing, spitting, hectic fever - *'ils meurent jeunes'*. Alcohol was another danger (although by no means particular to quarrymen): from Saint Goazec comes a Breton song in which the slate-worker promises Sainte Barbe, patron saint of the profession, that he'll stay sober all his life.

A study by pupils of the College of St-Trémeur in Carhaix includes testimony from many former quarry workers. Yves Flejou, who was born in Saint-Goazec in 1910, went to work in the Ardoisières du Rick at the age of thirteen and a half. His father had been killed whilst working in the same quarry when he was struck by a falling block. At that time, about twelve men worked at the extraction *au fond* and 20 *fendeurs* on the surface.

Pierre Brenner worked in quarries at Pont-Coblant (Stereon) from 1926 at the age of 15. He was given 'small tasks' until becoming a proper worker when he turned seventeen. Originally, work was paid by the task, but later in his career, the hours were set at 7 in the morning to 8 at night. He worked mostly as a *fendeur*, and describes the 'very repetitive and laborious work'. In fact, these men, prey to lumbago, were often left with permanently bent and disfigured backs from gruelling hours in an uncomfortable stance. His comrades who worked at the quarry face were all dead by 60 of silicosis, on account of inhaling the silica dust.

The slate he worked was generally for local use but some went further afield - for example, to Brest via Port-Launay. They made 18 varieties in different shapes and sizes: a speciality of the Pont-Coblant quarry was the *ardoise bretonne*, much in demand for repairing old roofs in Quimper. Altogether, the quarries supplied slate to Finistère, Côtes-du-Nord (now Côtes d'Armor) and Morbihan, but there was stiff competition from the mines of Anjou which served eastern

Brittany, and later from Spanish enterprises. The extent and richness of the Angevine mines finally proved too much for most small enterprises in the west of Brittany. Those at Pont-Coblant and St-Goazec were the most successful in Finistère, but transport by canal around the huge loops of the Aulne was too slow and costly to compete, and many seams had been fully exploited. The journey of 80 kilometres as the crow flies between Guily-Glas and Pontivy expanded to 153kms by canal. Most quarries struggled after 1914 and closed in the 1930s.

Soon after passing Rick quarry, the lock of Boudrac'h appears. Building stone for the château of Trévarez - a little way to the south - was unloaded at the dock here at the end of the 19th century. I know this spot well from a circular walk I offer once a year to my group. A regular sight-seeing boat 'manned' by a couple of competent, cheerful women is coming upstream so I cross the lock and passerelle and sit in the shade to watch their progress. The white dog lingers on the other side - have I finally thrown him off our scent? How easy it is to overestimate one's own importance! To my amazement, he hops on board the boat as it rises in the lock. This is obviously a regular party trick and he will presumably be put ashore back home nearly five kilometres away. So much for Brian's fatal attraction.

Rounding the long bend past Lock Boudrac'h, the last approach to Châteauneuf-du-Faou is fairly straight. The spire of the 19th century Chapelle de Notre-Dames-des-Portes soon appears dramatically high above the canal. A château once stood on this spur dominating the Aulne but it has long since disappeared: only the porch of its 15th century chapel can still be seen. It is worth breaking a journey to climb the steep slope to this pleasant hill-top town and have a look at the Pont-Aven school paintings by Paul Sérusier in the chapel of its other church of St-Julien. I continue along the canal past the ancient Pont du Roy (the King's bridge) and then the lock of Châteauneuf to yet another stretch of breath-taking fluvial scenery.

Chapter 9   Canal's End

"In the morning a man walks with his whole body;
in the evening, only with his legs"
                              Ralph Waldo Emerson

Today's walk begins at Kerbaouret, just beyond
Châteauneuf. Summer is well advanced here and the
Aulne valley glows warm and redolent, with richer redder
soil than the bleak scratchings of the *landes* and *tourbières*
(moor and peat-marsh) further north in the Monts d'Arrée.

Up high to the left the outline of the roofs of Trévarez is
soon apparent. An unusual angle for viewing this
comparatively modern château, conceived at the end of the
19th century by the Kerjegu family, and built of distinctive
red bricks which have earned it the familiar name of *château
rose*. Heartily bombed by the allies in 1944, when it was used
as a recuperation centre for wounded German U-boat men
and some Japanese submarine crew, the château
subsequently fell into disuse before a restoration programme
began after the Conseil Général of Finistère bought it in 1968.
Today it is famous for its gardens, a Breton Stourhead with
rhododendrons, camellias and azaleas the star turns. The
much older manor house, of simpler appeal, can be seen
beyond the chapel of St-Hubert, an animal-loving saint who
is also patron of the hunting fraternity. Beside the chapel are
some remarkable possibly prehistoric graves of local slate.

Just as impressive in its way is a house across the water
from the towpath with a cat-slide roof of incredible
proportions. A little further on, the opposite bank is a cloud
of wild garlic, which instantly conjures up childhood for me
and playing on the railway bank, a delightful tumble of wild
growth, behind the house where I was born, the house that
was my separate country in a complex conflict of identity.
Here along the waterside there is nothing but peace, the
silence and birdsong typical of the canal in Finistère.

As always, the first kilometre of a walk is a time of settling and regaining the sheer physical pleasure of walking. It takes a while to get into the rhythm of one's stride, which in itself then releases the brain for calmer reflection. So the mind and emotions quieten as the body does its natural work, obeying the most primitive instinct of man. Much later in the day will come the point where walking becomes hard-going physically and suddenly the body switches off auto-pilot and makes its own demands again.

This is truly a time for living in the moment, as nature burgeons all around, the promise inaugurated by Beltane, pagan festival of fire and fertility, now fulfilled. Who could fail to respond to the overtures of the land in summer, with all its sensual pleasure of growth and release? Borage blooms bright blue against a grey stone wall where a slip-road comes down from the main road. As I approach the old stone bridge before St-Thois, even the water seems full of life with its swirls and eddies, and the rippling evidence of movement in and under the banks as life gets going busily on a glorious day. It takes a sudden burst of traffic noise from the D72 to shatter the cocoon-like effect of the morning so far.

The Montagnes Noir or Black Mountains are more impressive at close range than from a distance. Their shelter makes the valley humid and it's certainly getting hotter by the minute as I pass trees dangling huge balls of mistletoe. I know this stretch of the canal well, as one of my guided walks follows the opposite bank and then meanders through the countryside around the pretty little bourg of St-Thois. It is clearly a long way from the last lock, as stagnant plugs of water are increasing to the right, natural run-off from fields that collects in the ditch below the level of the canal. The next lock will even things out.

As noisy jays flit about in the trees and raucous calls cross the water, a boat appears. It's a French family sailing downstream with a hire boat presumably from Aulne Loisirs at Châteauneuf. This is the first time this year I've seen human activity on the water, the utilization of the canal. *Pas grand chose*, but at least the water is in action. I catch up with them again soon after as they've moored before the next lock.

Their dog is tied up on the bank, causing Brian to run past in terror when it shows a snarly interest in him. The people greet us cheerily once more.

I'm thinking about integration again, having just refused an invitation to an event arranged by French people specially for the English. No-one seems to understand this, interpreting it as a form of ingratitude, which I find strange. The same things are unlikely to please everyone, and I didn't come to France to listen to French people telling me things I know already in English. I'd prefer to be told things I don't know in French, even if it can be a linguistic challenge sometimes, and I belong to various Breton organizations with historical interest. It's an odd dilemma for me. I run an association (with British and French members) for walking and exploring the history of Brittany: all the events are in English, because that is its purpose, making a closer relationship to their adopted land possible even for those who may struggle with the language. If you can't learn French to a level of easy understanding (and realistically that is true for many through no fault of their own), the wealth of Breton history is still accessible, and such understanding can be a powerful tool of integration. Personally I try to avoid any event with elements of tourist-speak and superficial or jokey level of presentation. I never enjoy the commonly built-in 'entertainment' factor of many events designed for foreigners, and prefer to stay away and be miserably serious on my own without spoiling anyone else's pleasure by carping criticisms. Now I call that unselfish.

For me, it's a shame when notions of Breton identity shrink to the size and shape of the ubiquitous korrigans, ugly images lauded as the essence of Breton culture for commercial gain. Brittany is not a quaint place, but a living reality with an endlessly varied landscape and rich repository of legends superseding the need for leprechaun substitutes. The identification with other 'celtic' cultures of Ireland, Wales and Cornwall reflects a shared ancestry, historical parallels and a mingled mass of legends derived from oral traditions.

I'm content to be part of a peaceful influx of Britons into Brittany again, a new historic wave of settlement, but to be part of an invasion, an intrusion is different. When the invader seeks to impose or to demand his own culture the prospect is repellent. And I equally deplore the commercial values that lead French supermarkets to provide shelves of British products. Britons have plenty to offer here - their initiative, enterprise and energy are helpful to the local economy both in terms of innovation with new businesses and in supporting those already in existence. Many thousands of British people simply live quietly in Brittany without the need for external trappings of Englishness. I cannot and never will see the value of recreating an English lifestyle in another country. We are not tourists but inhabitants, a very different role and social identity.

I am now passing farms at regular intervals on the north side of the canal and quiet little enclaves of old granite/schist houses side-by-side with modern hangars, and white rendered 20th century Breton homes, occasionally a whole complex in ruin not yet offered for sale as a potential gîte project. Sullen fishermen people the locks, and plants beside the towpath are spattered with oil where someone has been resurfacing part of the path without much care.

At Ty Men I stop for a rest and to look at an old canal relic, the *chaland* Victor. An association was formed in 2003 to preserve and restore this canal barge, and its metal hull remains on show on the canal bank. The boat was built in Nantes in 1893 and bought by Nicolas Le Page from Port-Launay. Its cargo was to be fertilizer for farms along the valley, with slate quarry products collected for the return journey at Carhaix, Saint-Goazec, Châteauneuf and Pont-Coblant.

An accident in 1932 put an end to this career, when Victor collided with one of the piles of the bridge at Ty Men in a strong current, despite the efforts of the *batelier* with his horse to save it. The boat was emptied of cargo and then hauled up to rest under the bank opposite the towpath. Forty years seems not bad service on Victor's part, then languishing in the water for 70 years before the campaign to 'Save Victor' from total disintegration began. I can't help thinking it's rather like putting an old person in a home and trying to keep them alive whatever the cost when they'd rather have died quietly and with dignity in their own natural element.

A group of elderly people start walking along the canal from Ty Men to a well-placed seat. Another elderly man on a bike passes. This is the perfect recreation and relaxation for those over the age of easy physical exercise. It is also a place of memory for many - no-one it seems is without a fragment of memory of the canal - childhood games, romantic dalliance, quiet contemplation - some little place in their life filled by its stoical flow and verdant setting. The richness and value of its human experience has continued well after its useful economic life. I hope that the inevitable tourist development won't cheapen this and reduce it to a string of rubbish bins, plastic seats and colourful notice-boards of frivolous interpretation.

The day begins to deteriorate as yet again that sudden agonizing pain shoots through my lower calf. It's a really odd sensation, on the surface of the skin, but with a seering intensity that makes walking almost unbearable. The next three kilometres pass extremely slowly and bitterly as I try to practise the 'feel into the pain' method of healing which helps only marginally. These huge sweeping bends, usually so attractive, now make my heart sink as they only emphasise the distance to Pont-Coblant. When I do finally stagger to my waiting car I discover that my tape-recorder is jammed and the last couple of hours of notes are lost. But as soon as I take off my sock, the pain in my leg disappears.

Another day I continue the walk with an early morning start, having driven over the Monts d'Arrée in mist that presages a hot and probably muggy day. At Pont-Coblant lorries are using the towpath for access to a noisy construction site, but past the bridge things soon get quieter. The former quarry of Stereon is on the right, as slate heaps still testify. At the lock further on, a worker died in an explosion in 1824, a reminder

113

of the essentially dangerous work of canal construction. Brutally, there was no compensation for families in these circumstances.

A swan shelters under foliage where the trees hang low over the water and lime trees enhance a graceful bend. On the other side of river two magnificent chestnut trees are in blossom by a crop-filled field and, beyond, a hamlet with ruined houses covered in ivy. Farm machinery drones constantly and a tractor jolts up and down in another field, the activity contrasting with the peaceful wooded slopes on my side of the towpath. Round another bend and there is a deafening moment of quiet, trees looming high and tall and vigorous, the farmland now behind a screen of shrubbier versions.

Insect life is vibrant and with that intensity peculiar to their species. Wings beat the air into light trails around my face and something lands on my nose as I try to take a photograph of the towpath. It's interesting that despite all the people who can name trees or flowers or birds by the hundred, I have never met an insect-lover, someone both passionate and reverent about these buzzy, leggy nuisances. I fear that insects must play their crucial part in the balance of nature with little appreciation for their efforts.

Up ahead are some workmen. One chap is on his mobile phone, getting advice by the way he keeps gesticulating at a shallow trench in the bank; the other is a young man with his back to my approach. He jumps in surprise as I come level with him and then grins at his own reaction. The other man greets me too as I pass. Brian is too scared to follow me past them and hangs back, then rushes forward to safety to the men's great amusement. I realize that friendly contact is the norm in these circumstances, when we are physically on the same level and look each other, as humans, in the eye. We share the same small piece of earth and are clearly cut, roughly speaking, from the same cloth. But put someone inside the protective and isolating metal box of a car or van, or high up on a tractor and it's a different story. The vehicle has become a great separating device in this modern world where more divides than unites us. A cyclist comes up behind without me hearing him and looks at me strangely. Only later do I realize that as he couldn't see the tape recorder in my hand, he must have thought I was talking to myself.

A very pretty lock-house with a well-kept garden has an English name on the postbox. Light shimmers so strongly on the lock that it looks like a huge flashing silver neon sign when looking back. Bright sunshine and ripples on the water cause the reflections of the trees to shimmer in a moving tableau of great beauty.

The scenery now opens out a bit, with a low hill on the other side, and a long meadow to my right. Along the towpath, many new young ash trees have been planted. I hope to see them tall and proud in twenty years time. A few brave clovers have escaped the carnage of the verge cutting.

A seat presents itself in the perfect spot for a rest and it is very quiet after a lone light aircraft has passed over. Both the air and the water smell fresh and clean, and breathing is as good as a draught from a spring. Two dogs, presumably tethered on farms, one on each side of the valley, keep up an occasional conversation of coded barks, alerting each other to the presence of humans in the no-man's land between their territories. Or maybe they are just exchanging the time of day to relieve their boredom.

I eventually continue in full sun on a very exposed long stretch, past the lock at Lothey, which has an enviable house, and then with the church of Vieux-Bourg visible across the river. A crow rises up out of the middle of a field of long grass, attracting Brian who is instantly alert for the chase, but doesn't jump the ditch. The bird flaps off nonchalantly. These big birds are so casual, so confident of their strength and aggression. It reminds me of an incident with Rufus, my beloved lurcher, at Glastonbury when his speed and intelligence were more than a match for the crow who hadn't bargained for that in a dog. Rufus actually caught the crow on the rise - for a split second of uncertainty Rufus, the crow and I all wondered whether the bird would fall, but it dragged itself away, leaving the dog with a mouthful of wing feathers.

Just before the next lock, is a scene that could be a snapshot of perfection. There is a dew-pond to the right in a meadow in a small depression: one small and one large oak tree shade it. It's a natural still-life, a moment hard to hold on to and one that would be enhanced by a visiting cow or horse, but completely spoilt by human presence. The countryside was once the natural milieu for the vast majority of the population: now we herd.

I lunch under a shady tree with the sound of the N164 just above and find myself wondering about ID cards, which are being discussed as a possibility in England. Those against the system have an easy argument in 'big brother' scare-mongering, but in these days of instant access anything, the information is out there anyway. The ID card seems to me a formalization of an existing state of affairs and I wonder if there has ever been a fuss in France about it? Here there doesn't seem to be that sense that the French are affronted that anyone wants to know about them. In banks, for example, I've been routinely asked questions about my work and status that I would never have been asked (or if so would have refused to answer) in England. But I've always felt the French in general to be confident of who they are and their place in the community or social identity, a concept their whole administrative and political system is designed to generate. The 'liberty' of the French revolution was not about individualism, although equality and fraternity are perhaps relevant to the ID card issue. In England people's resistance to the idea of ID cards may be based ultimately on an insecurity of individual identity as much as a fear of state control. 'The Englishman's home is his castle' is a not a notion that sits easily in France.

Setting off again, I find it unpleasantly hot for walking now even though a tense breeze is getting up and branches begin to creak and groan around me. As I stop to listen to the wind whispering through a stand of poplar trees opposite, a mysterious shimmer runs across the surface of the water and then disappears as if a moving spirit had passed over.

The landscape on the other side of the canal is yet again dominated by cultivated land and a massive farm-complex, which seems characteristic of the Montagnes Noires. It's a poor comparison with the wild and free terrain of the Monts d'Arrée not far to the north. At least on the towpath side I have the pleasure of meeting a handsome and personable Frenchman at the lock of Le Guillec.

What seems an age later, past slatey banks and the Ecluse de l'Aulne with its islands and caravans, I finally pass under the bridge of the Brest to Quimper motorway to some gracious shade and an exceptional display of varied trees on the huge towering hillside opposite. The water is calm, wide and green, butterflies are everywhere. Out of the blazing sun in this deep valley it is possible to enjoy the characteristics of the season.

The use of the canal was once well-regulated, as would be expected of French administration. A little booklet of 'Police du Canal' rules issued by the department of Finistère in 1897 lays down the law for such practicalities as the height and width of boats, the size of letters with which the name and home of the owner must be displayed (at least 8cms), the lighting for night-sailing, passing etiquette and how to park the boats, whilst also minutely detailing required paperwork. A long list of forbidden behaviour including throwing anything into the water.

Water is a highly political issue in Finistère, where the conflicting interests of farmers and consumers, fishermen and tourists vie vociferously in the corridors of power. Everyone has an axe to grind, but the political and commercial muscle of the agricultural community has a very loud voice. The argument that economic development is the only way forward for protection of the region's watercourses is as full of holes as a leaking *rigole*. Uncontaminated rivers are vital not only for the production of drinking water but also for the ecological health of the area. Water entering the canal often has high nitrate content to begin with and the large stagnant areas between locks are a factor in further

117

deterioration. Water quality, and therefore the whole environment, is damaged by the practices of intensive modern farming. That's the bottom line, and significant swift changes are blocked by recalcitrance, despite many initiatives such as SAGE (*Schéma d'aménagement et de gestion des eaux*) to broker agreements of benefit to all partners. Gradual improvement must be the objective to fulfil European directives on water quality, supported by courageous political action.

I'm physically quite tired now on this hot summer day but the long loops of the Aulne with widening views on either side make for gentle walking. At the next lock, Prat-Hir, a low stone wall provides a perch to watch crows turning over pickings in a ploughed field, as two cheerful cyclists sail by. There are palm trees and hydrangeas planted on the canal bank and the house with its sun-porch would not be out of place in Surrey. The next lock too has a very prettified house and 'window' boxes on the lock gates. This is starting to feel like the last leg of a marathon journey.

On the way into Châteaulin there is a big and noisy industrial plant to pass. A fisherman on the bank is oblivious, absorbed in his calm, self-contained past-time. He has some pleasant shade too, as large horse-chestnut trees overhang the towpath throwing out pools of deep cool shadow, and even extend right out over the water. I have the cynical thought that the next time I come along here they'll probably have been cut down.

The heat is oppressive now and the curve of the river deceptive. I keep thinking I must be nearly there and long for the sight of the ancient chapel of Notre-Dame perched up on the opposite hill, but the exposed path seems relentless. Marker stone 359 is now behind me, so it can't be far. The river looks very brown and murky.

Lots of young people just out of school or college are sitting on seats by the canal. Traffic whizzes along on a road on the opposite bank. Back to busy 'civilisation' and it's quite a shocking contrast as I stagger on, red-faced and sweaty. More and more people appear on the towpath - groups of elderly people with little dogs, an old woman, smartly dressed and made-up, with a walking stick, sitting on a bench. An aura of loneliness surrounds her, but she gives a wide, warm smile that eases my weariness and bucks me up for the last gruelling stretch of a day that has turned into a bit of an endurance test.

Châteaulin is a place it took me years to appreciate. It's busy, with the river cutting through the middle and rows of shops and restaurants on either side so that the waterside is part of the life of the town. One low road bridge and one high curving one unite the two parts. The earliest settlement (and a château long since disappeared) was on the far bank, perched high above the Aulne. Some extremely ancient houses survive up there around the Chapelle de Notre-Dame, which is well worth the climb, with its enclosure containing triumphal arch, ossuary and weathered calvaire. The latter is made of Kersanton granite and depicts an unusual choice of subject in the last judgement on its east face.

Châteaulin has long been famous for salmon, which feature in the town coat-of-arms. 'Penn Eog' (salmon head) is a sometime epithet for the inhabitants, in the same way as Penn Sardin was used of people from Douarnenez. In 1090 Alain Fergent, duke of Brittany, gave fishing rights in the Aulne to the downstream abbey of Landévennec. In the 17th century they came into the possession of the king of France, when salmon became the *poisson royal*. It was said one could catch up to 100 salmon per day here: that sort of boast even brought fishermen from Hungary to Châteaulin before WWII. Englishman John Kemp came to this area in the mid-19th century, expecting a thriving town but finding Châteaulin to be 'an insignificant village' of about 1800 inhabitants. In his book on shooting and fishing in Brittany he describes starting by the first lock at 4am with a French companion who catches then loses a fine salmon. Kemp says that he saw many fish trying to mount the water chute beside that lock without success. (Earlier in his trip he had found the Blavet at Pontivy, once a great fishing river, ruined for that purpose by the canalization.)

Today I continue straight on through the town along the

canal, passing the lock and the *passe à poissons* where the fish can be seen beneath the water level. The long stretch out to Port-Launay is unprepossessing and dominated by an awareness of traffic, but on arrival the old harbour with its genteel, slightly faded charm more than makes up for it. Round the last bend the final lock of the canal at Guily-Glas is only a kilometre ahead, just under the lofty railway viaduct, whose arches span the water.

At the lock there is a new state-of-the-art barrage regulating the powerful flow of the Aulne by means of three great valves controlled by sensors. I had understood that the enormous cost and effort of building this sleek trapping across the river was a response to the serious flooding problem, which as recently as 2000 left many homes and businesses under several metres of water. But maybe I was wrong - at the first hint of rising waters in 2008 an article appeared in the press suggesting that the barrage was not intended as an anti-flood measure. In England they would say 'it's the wrong sort of flood'.

A Breton friend used to play here by the lock near his grand-aunt's home. She ran a small café/épicerie, and during the German occupation, supplemented her income to support family refugees from Paris by poaching fish from the Aulne. She once gave her sister a salmon to deliver to a contact in Châteaulin. Going by bicycle, the young woman nervously passed the check-point in Port-Launay safely, only to be stopped nearer the town and questioned about the wrapped parcel. 'Is it a torpedo?' the German soldiers jested. The salmon was quickly confiscated on discovery and a bank-note tossed into the basket. On reaching home she tore the money up, saying *'Je ne veux pas vivre de l'argent des Boches'*.

Technically I have now reached the end of the canal, more than 360kms from the beginning of the towpath all the way back at Quiheix. I sit quietly on a bench for a while, re-running that long route in my mind. There's no doubt I feel calmer and clearer about issues that have occupied my long thoughts on this staggered trek. There's been some emotional movement, a realisation that since living in Brittany my own personal concept of identity has developed from the external to the internal. There are depths to draw on, tendrils wedging themselves in crevices of the moist earth.

But the journey isn't quite over yet.

Chapter 10   On to Brest

"The journey is the reward"
Chinese Proverb

After the last lock at Guily-Glas, a track continues along the free-flowing river for several hundred metres. This is a different quality of experience from canal-walking as the Aulne seems to sense the release of its chains and powers towards the Rade de Brest. Summer is over and as I walk in the rain and muggy atmosphere, vapour rises from the woods across the water in puffs, as if a giant were pipe-smoking under the trees. The wind hisses in the reeds as hunters' guns fire and the sound of a chainsaw starting up echoes like a reverberating fart.

The path soon joins the road uphill to the remarkable Chapelle de Saint-Sébastien, placed in a look-out position dominating the Aulne valley. Technically part of the commune of Saint-Ségal, it is out on a limb, separated from the bourg by the Quimper/Brest motorway. An aura of peaceful calm hangs over the old settlement around the church, which, with its Breton Baroque interior (dating mainly from the 17th century) was probably built originally for protection against the plague or in gratitude for the locality being spared its ravages. Swirling patterns grace the honeyed Logonna stone masonry: by contrast the base of the mid-16th century calvary is in dark Kersanton, four moon-like faces decorating each façade. On the triumphal arch, two archers, one nonchalantly hand on hip, fire their arrows at the saint.

Beyond this point there is no easy route to follow: it is necessary to get past the motorway which crosses the estuary of the Douffine, so I opt for a lift via Pont-de-Buis-lès-Quimerc'h to pick up minor roads at Logonna-Quimerc'h and then forest tracks along the wooded banks of the Aulne - back in tidal waters, the path is not always passable. High above is the Belvedere at Rosnoën from which vantage point the incredible loops of the river can be seen like an aerial photograph. From here the GR34-37 leads to the only remaining fixed crossing point of the Aulne which replaced the earlier ferry between Térénez and Landévennec.

The Pont de Térénez is a suspension bridge connecting the mainland with the Presqu'île de Crozon, a peninsula nothing like an island in fact, despite having a distinct atmosphere of its own. The bridge was built in the 1920s and then destroyed by the Germans in 1944. Rebuilt, it finally opened again in 1952 and today is badly in need of retirement - a new bridge is currently being constructed alongside with the intended opening date of 2010. There is an information and presentation centre for this mammoth task on the right bank hillside above the works, in one of the numerous temporary office buildings around the site.

After crossing the Pont de Térénez, one is now forced to follow an alternative route to Moulin-Mer whilst the new bridge is under construction (a great pity as the old path directly there along the Aulne is one of my favourites). It's a pleasant enough route, however, back along the river bank, apparently in completely the wrong direction, then up over the hillside, across the main road, and down through the Forêt de Landévennec to a deep inlet by the old mill. Walking up to the head of the estuary in light rain, I come to the Chapelle du Folgoat.

Set in an idyllic spot this little chapel commemorates the legend of the simpleton (Fol) Salaun who lived alone in these woods, with trees and birds for his friends, fed by charity, and able to say only the words Ave Maria. When he died and was buried on this spot, a wonderful lily bloomed bearing the same two words: on investigation it was found to be sprouting from the mouth of his body. After this miracle, the abbot of Landévennec had the first chapel built here in 1645. A later version remains today, with the story told in strikingly simple stained glass windows. The same legend is also attached to Le Folgoët (Fool's Wood) in northern Finistère.

After another long stretch through the undulating forest, with its rocky outcrops and dense hush, like a scene from a lost world, the path mounts steeply to the D60 and back into quiet rural reality. Soon after, a fork to the right meanders down a residential road towards the bourg of Landévennec. On the way a viewing point affords a bird's eye view of the ships' graveyard in the Aulne channel and the sombre Ile de Térénez. After another kilometre or so, the entrance to the modern abbey is to the right. It's possible to visit the church and a large shop selling books, cards and sweets made on the premises, but I go there often enough to research in the historical library so instead I continue downhill and turn right at the bottom of the road to the exceptional site of the ancient ruins and an evocative museum.

The first abbey was built on the shore of the Aulne in the 5th century by St-Guénolé, who had originally settled with his monks on the inhospitable island of Tibidy where they were battered by the winds and storms. From there across an expanse of open water into which the great river Aulne flowed they could see a 'magnificent forest, and hollowed from its midst a deep valley facing the rising sun.' This account from the 9th century life of St-Guénolé by the monk Gurdisten describes the grass is greener syndrome to good effect: 'from the bottom of the valley every day just after sunrise, a mist rose like smoke and to those who saw the place it seemed the most pleasant place there ever was. They wanted nothing more than to be taken there.' It only required the formality of a miracle with the waters parting at the touch of Guénolé's staff, for them to hop across and set up home in this more salubrious environment.

The earliest abbey founded by Guénolé has vanished without trace, but plenty of evidence of the Carolingian version in the 9th century remains, although a more elaborate church dates from the 12/13th centuries. It became an important centre of learning, in the Benedictine tradition, as the works on view in the museum there today bear witness. Illuminated manuscripts present the conventional subjects of saints' lives and the gospels but also a great range of wider spheres of knowledge from medicine to astronomy. The abbey's Cartulaire, an 11th century document, like that of Redon, collects together the charters of ownership governing abbey lands, a vast patchwork of property that was a great source of wealth for the abbey.

Standing near the shore today it is not hard in a time-slip of imagination to see Viking ships forge ominously to the shore. In 913 they appeared at Landévennec and the abbey was sacked and fired, although it seems likely that the monks had enough warning to get away with their greatest treasures in time. They did not return to the site at Landévennec for fifty years. In the succeeding centuries it fared little better in conflicts from the Wars of Religion to the French Revolution. Becoming National Property (like all abbeys) at the end of the 18th century, the monastery and its estate were eventually sold off. In private hands it became a source of building material. One fact serves to illustrate that the days of great abbeys were well and truly over: the cloister designed by Robert Plouvier in the 17th century ended up as part of the chicken market at Brest.

Something of a revival in the abbey's fortunes came in the latter part of the 19th century when the Comte de Chalus bought what was left of the property with a view to restoration and preservation. He also planted many of the palm trees that are now a common feature of the little bourg. The Benedictines took over again in the 1950s and built the new abbey higher up the hillside with breathtaking views over the entrance to the Aulne estuary. In keeping with their traditions of study and scholarship, the Bibliothèque Bretonne is today an invaluable source for reference and research.

Wandering on down to the shore, I feast my eyes on the channel leading to the Rade of Brest, regarded by many as the finest roadstead in the world. This remarkable natural harbour of 150km², well sheltered from Atlantic storms, provides both an alluring refuge for a fleet but also a potential trap, an aspect exploited to the full by the English in the 18th and early 19th centuries. Napoleon's letters in 1806 reveal his frustration with a recalcitrant commander who refused to get out from the Fort de Berthaume and along the channel of the Goulet to attack the English fleet hovering in the Atlantic, despite a superiority of numbers. One excuse followed another, but he stayed put and even Napoleon himself baulked at giving the decisive command before his attention was diverted by more pressing matters. In the commander's defence, it is true that making speedy headway out into the Atlantic in the face of prevailing westerlies is not the easiest of tasks, even for modern shipping, the funnel shape of the connecting passage of water exacerbating the effects of both winds and currents.

The Rade is like an inland sea, its sheer size hard to take in because from any one vantage point the view is limited by promontories, islands and peninsulas, a jumble of angles and changing shapes. A map gives only an overall mechanical view. An aerial photograph is more indicative of the scope and shape of this natural resource but cannot convey the spirit of the Rade. For that one needs, at best, to venture out onto its gently ruffled surface, but just to stand and stare and imagine is almost as good. The calm waters belie what it might hold or sustain: teams of boats still search for old bombs in these depths.

The view of the city of Brest itself is obscured by the Pointe d'Armorique, with its fenced military installation. There is not yet any continuous coastal path around the peninsulas hemming the Rade, so transport to this particular point may be necessary. From the little round car-park near the fenced-off zone, a scenic path leads to the nearby Pointe de Caro where one is faced by the great port of western Brittany just across the water, and the Goulet de Brest, squeezing at its narrowest point between the Pointe des Espagnols and the Pointe du Portzic. The sight is redolent of the varied past fortunes in these waters. The Rade with its visual reminders of Vauban's late 17th century protective chain of forts and the atmospheric lilt of its shimmering surface - light and shade, hope and despair, life and death - cannot fail to trigger the historical imagination.

In 1513 at the mouth of the Goulet a resounding explosion took the Cordelière to the bottom of the sea together with its English foe. This great ship was built near Morlaix for Anne, Duchess of Brittany, and had already seen much successful active service. Lying in the Rade with other Breton ships, the crew and passengers were celebrating the Feast of St-Laurent when the English fleet appeared. A hard fought contest ensued, particularly with the English vessels Souverain and Regent, the latter commanded by Thomas Kernevet. The Souverain was rendered hors de combat, whilst the Regent in flight was pursued and attached with grappling irons. Fighting ranged over the decks and, what happened next is subject to various interpretations. According to Breton tradition, the commander of the Cordelière, Hervé de Portzmorguer, realising defeat was inevitable, deliberately fired his powder store to blow up both ships. He is said to have noted the appropriateness of this action on the day of St-Laurent who also died by fire, according to legend having called out to his torturers as they barbecued him to turn him over as his first side was done.

The most chilling image of the Rade is that of U-boats cutting like sharks through the water on their secret missions of subterfuge, in and out of the pens at Brest during WWII. The Germans arrived in the city in June 1940 and soon began work on the submarine base. This secure housing of the thickest concrete withstood fierce allied bombing raids for years until August 1944, when Lancasters of 617 squadron were able to inflict serious damage with the new Tallboy bombs. Meanwhile most of the rest of the city had been flattened into oblivion to be later replaced - of necessity swiftly to re-house the population - by the unlovely conurbation it is today.

I reach the great port across the old bridge, Pont Albert Louppe, which runs parallel to the motorway across the impressive Elorn estuary. In Brest at the end of my journey I come back to the beginning, the original motivation for money to pour into the bottomless pit of canal construction between Nantes and Brest. Brest's strategic importance as an Atlantic port, a naval building centre and the site of an extensive arsenal were all good reasons for connection and a reliable supply line with Lorient and Nantes, as the supremacy of the British navy and their blockading tactics threatened Napoleon's ambitions.

Brest developed late as a centre of major importance despite its enviable position straddling the Penfeld estuary. Originally, a stronghold of the Osismes tribe and then a Roman *castellum*, it became the possession of the Comtes de Léon until the 13th century when Hervé III, in financial straits, sold the château, port and town to Jean I Le Roux (Red-haired), duke of Brittany. In the wars of succession a hundred years later, Brest was taken and held for nearly fifty years by the English, who backed Jean de Montfort's claims to the dukedom. Richard II returned the town to Brittany in 1397.

It was Cardinal Richlieu, governor of Brittany from 1626, who was the first to develop the potential of the city he called *'mon Brest'*, decreeing that it was to become the military port for the Atlantic seaboard. In 1681 Brest replaced St-Renan as the regional capital: the document signed by Louis XIV to effect this significant change is on display in the Tour Tanguy, a restored 14th century tower on the west bank of the Penfeld. This now houses a museum of the history of Brest, including vivid reconstructions of old street scenes and the famous ship Cordelière.

It was inevitable that Vauban, royal engineer par excellence, should have had a hand in the construction of Brest's defensive systems between 1683 and 1695. He described the city as *'un port royal, pourvu de tous les avantages qu'on sauroit désirer, et d'une manière aussi complète que si Dieu avait prit plaisir à le faire exprès.'* Construction of the batteries around the goulet and canon emplacements in the château were carried out under his auspices.

In the mid-18th century, local man Choquet de Lindu was responsible for later projects such as development of the arsenal. This was particularly important to military plans, a large-scale enterprise employing as many as 5000 people before the revolution. Workshops, forges and warehouses stretched along both sides of the Penfeld estuary; ship-building, fitment and armaments created a hive of activity - as shown in contemporary paintings - and from this creative nest came ships that sailed across the Atlantic to seal the Americans' bid for independence from the British with a decisive intervention at Chespeake Bay in 1781.

In 1750 de Lindu built the *bagne* (prison), a vast establishment housing hundreds of men who were used as labour in the arsenal. Convicts from here were sent to construct the Grande Tranchée of the Nantes-Brest canal at Glomel. When the prison was closed a hundred years later the alternative 'punishment' of shipping criminals to the colonies was employed.

The ancient château at Brest, strategically placed above the Penfeld estuary, remarkably survived the pounding by allied bombers which reduced most of the rest of the city to rubble. Its impregnable position impressed even the great warrior de Guesclin, who thought it not worth bothering to try a siege in 1373. Today the staunch medieval towers overlook activity on the river and in the Rade, and contain a well-executed maritime museum.

Opposite the château is the Cours Dajot, a promenade built by prisoners from the *bagne*, which provides a panoramic view overlooking the Rade. It seems a good place for last thoughts on this project, a calm ending to a long search. The canal does not actually reach Brest any more than it starts in Nantes and perhaps I've no more arrived at a final answer to my niggling questions of identity. But this journey has brought me a much clearer awareness of my attachment to this adopted land and a realization that personal identity for me is much about comfort of surroundings and a sense of fitness within the landscape. Most of this walking time I have spent alone, a state of affairs that seems increasingly natural. The sense of my separate selves has not changed but they are living together in greater harmony, and I've acquired a closer connection between being and belonging.

That there can be a distinction between one's homeland and the place where one belongs is the golden nugget mined by this long journey. My error for many years has been to assume these two shangri-las to be of necessity the same, which tinged my experiences in England with the drab colours of failure. Whilst I admire and envy those for whom two such stabilizing factors coalesce, it is a liberation to accept finally that there is an alternative path to follow, and it is one that can provide equally firm footholds. Finistère, the end of the earth, far-flung outpost of the Roman empire, a rude desert for the Parisian administration has become a home for me and the beginning of a new way of being: an acceptance of my individuality unbolstered by family and traditions.

This journey has anchored me firmly in the landscape and history of my adopted, and who knows, perhaps my ancestral country. I don't think I'll bother resorting to past life regression in the hope of discovering that in a previous existence I was a celtic princess or arch druid. There's no need for fantasy: I feel the bond in the reality of now. For me the key to this is walking, to place myself physically in the context of a land and all its historical connections, for history is the soil around the fragile roots of identity. Anyone involved in the futile pursuit of definition of identity must come ultimately to the temptation of Alexander's solution when faced with the complexities of the Gordian knot. Slash through the externals, and identity is visceral not mental, capable of neither measure nor calculation. It is time to trust in an intuitive sense of belonging and the realisation that personal identity for me is a landscape not a language, and its solidity matches the ground beneath my feet as I walk.

The canal, has given me many things, from faithful company to historical lessons and a delphic path of exploration. This may be the end of the long thought but a new road is always just ahead. For me walking is being, and where I walk is who I am.

We shall not cease from exploration
And the end of all our exploring
Will be to arrive where we started
And know the place for the first time.

T.S.Eliot - Four Quartets

Further interest

The Canal

Le Canal – A pied de Nantes à Brest by Thierry Guidet
(Editions UBACS)

Les Bagnards du canal de Nantes à Brest by Jean Kergrist
(Keltia Graphic)

Le Canal de Nantes à Brest by Kader Benferhat & Sandra Aubert
(Editions Ouest-France)

Walking

Wanderlust - A History of Walking by Rebecca Solnit
(Verso)

Brittany

Discovering the History of Brittany by Wendy Mewes
(Red Dog Books)

Websites

www.canaux-bretons.net

www.brittanywalks.com

Acknowledgements

Grateful thanks to all those canal folk - walkers, workers, fishers, officials, authors, animals - who have helped me on this journey.

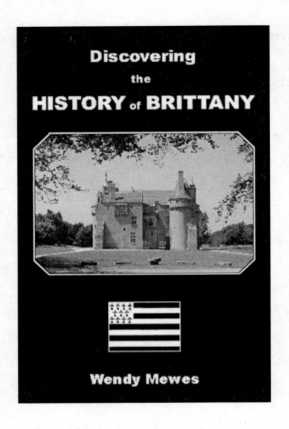

Discovering the History of Brittany
by Wendy Mewes
(ISBN 978 0 9536001 5 1)
£8.99 or 13@50

available on line
www.reddogbooks.com

Distributed in Brittany by Coop Breizh
(see www.reddogbooks.com for list of stockists)

Also available through any good UK bookseller